Introduction

Fire
IN THE
Desert

Becoming a Habitation for His Presence

ANGELA G. WALKER

Fire in the Desert

FIRE IN THE DESERT: Becoming a Habitation For His Presence

© Dr Angela G Walker 2021
First Edition

All rights reserved.
No part of this publication may be reproduced or transmitted in any form or by any means, electronic or mechanical, including photocopying, recording or any information storage and retrieval system, without prior permission in writing from the author.

Unless stated otherwise, scripture quotations are taken from the Holy Bible New International Version (NIV) Bible. © 1973, 1978, 1984 by International Bible Society.

Scripture marked 'NASB' are taken from the New American Standard Bible®. Copyright © 1960, 1962, 1963, 1968, 1971, 1972, 1973, 1975, 1977, 1995 by The Lockman Foundation.
Scripture marked 'NKJV' are taken from the New King James Version. Copyright © 1982 by Thomas Nelson, Inc.
Scripture quotations marked 'TPT' are taken from The Passion Translation. Copyright © 2014 by BroadStreet Publishing.

Cover Artist: Rebecca Priestley
Cover Graphics: Caroline Bishop

ISBN: 9798695304046

Introduction

Acknowledgements

I would like to thank Rachel Gray for proofreading the book, Becky Priestly for her prophetic art, and Caroline Bishop for her graphic design on the cover. Thank you all for you amazing contributions and talents in helping to release this book.

Dedication

I dedicate this book to my Mum and Dad, who have inspired and supported me in my spiritual journey with God, especially during the wilderness or desert seasons. Thank you for your faith and spiritual discernment that encouraged me not to give up but to keep moving forward, trusting in Him.

Contents

Introduction   7

1 Deeper Still 13
2 Metamorphosis 31
3 His Resting Place 39
4 Overcoming Circumstances 53
5 Refiner's Fire 71
6 Highway of Holiness 87
7 Spiritual Breakthrough 97
8 Growing in Grace 111
9 Promotion in the Wilderness 121
10 From Outer Court to Bridal Chamber 137
11 His Burning Ones 155
12 Tabernacles of His Glory 169

Conclusion 181
Appendix A: *By the Author* 183
Appendix B: *About the Author* 189

Prayer of Surrender

Lord Jesus, I surrender my *body* to You

I give You my desires, strengths and abilities. I surrender my senses – what I see, hear, smell, feel and taste. Lord, cleanse my senses with Your sanctifying blood, so I may see, hear, discern and sense things in the Spirit. Speak Lord, what You want to say to my spirit.

Lord Jesus, I surrender my *soul* to You

I surrender my mind, will and emotions, and also my imagination to You. Lord, cleanse my thoughts, feelings and imagination with Your blood. Filter what comes in and goes out, in my conscious, subconscious and unconscious. Teach me how to discern Your ways and Your will.

Lord Jesus, I surrender my *spirit* to You

Lord Jesus, cleanse and sanctify my spirit, so my spirit may be one with You. Teach me how to move in Your Spirit and live a Spirit-led life.

Lord, I offer my body, soul and spirit to You as a living sacrifice (Romans 12:1). Lead me by Your Spirit and transform my heart, so I may follow You all the days of my life.

Introduction

Many of us may experience desert or wilderness seasons at some point in life, where God seems distant and we feel alone, confused, or don't know where we are going. Some may refer to it as the 'dark night of the soul'.

I believe there are various reasons for the desert seasons we encounter, and the purpose of this book is to help you through such seasons, and draw you closer to the heart of God.

Desert seasons can be divine opportunities for God to transform our hearts, and also to develop a much deeper faith and hunger for His presence.

Sometimes, a breakthrough may be the thing that is required to take us deeper in our relationship with God. During such seasons we may fast and pray, since fasting is a power tool for spiritual breakthrough. It is when we pursue Him with all our hearts that we will find Him, and come into union with Him. *'You will seek Me and find Me, when you seek Me with all your heart,'* (Jeremiah 29:13).

Fire in the Desert

For some, the wilderness is a time of 'transition' where the Holy Spirit leads us out of the 'familiar' and into something 'unfamiliar'. Transition seasons may last for months or years, depending on the response in our hearts. During such seasons, we let go of the old so He may prepare our hearts to embrace the new. This may be a time of training for reigning, as we see in the lives of Joseph, Moses, David, Esther, and Jesus Himself. The spiritual desert is a perfect place for God to prepare our hearts to step into His purposes and divine callings.

Hence, the desert is the ideal place where God can withdraw us from the influences and distractions of this world, so our hearts may focus on Him. It is like climbing our personal mountain with the Lord. It is a step by step process as we learn to tune our spirit into hearing His gentle voice. Our baggage becomes lighter, as we learn to surrender the areas of our heart to Him. The further we progress up the mountain, the lighter the load, as we let go of our carnal nature and the ways of the world.

Desert seasons may be short or long, depending on our heart's response and willingness to surrender to His Spirit. The most important thing is to keep pressing deeper, as we pursue His presence.

Sometimes, the desert can be compared to the 'chrysalis' phase of a butterfly. This is a time where He takes us through a process of spiritual transformation in our hearts. It is the season where we let go of our old self, including habits, attitudes and mindsets, so our hearts may become transformed from an earth-bound or carnal lifestyle, into a Kingdom and Spirit-led lifestyle.

In 2018, the Lord spoke to me about 'corporate transformation'. I was wondering how He could bring about a corporate transformation in the body of Christ. Then in 2020, something happened that was going to change the nations. It was the

Introduction

outbreak of the Corona virus, *Covid 19,* and this caused the nations to go in lockdown, to prevent the further spread of the virus. People were ordered to stay at home and not go to work unless necessary. Businesses shut, schools were closed, restaurants and hotels stopped functioning, the entertainment and sports industry ceased, and even churches were forced to close their doors.

However, for some this 'lockdown' season became an opportunity for 'corporate transformation' in the homes, families, businesses and even churches. It was a time for recalibration and realignment, as people focused their hearts on God and pursued more of His presence.

The purpose of this book is to encourage you through the desert, so you may draw closer to the heart of God. I pray it is a time to stop what you are doing, look into His eyes, engage in His presence and listen to Him. Instead of turning back, continue to press forward, as you let His Spirit lead you step by step of the way.

God has amazing plans for you that are far bigger than you can imagine. We simply have to give Him our reins of control as we submit to the reign of His Spirit in our hearts. As we allow God to transform our hearts and minds, we can become one of His beautiful hand-carved vessels, through which the Father may display His fire and His glory.

This journey is one to be embraced and enjoyed, until our hearts become a place of habitation for Him. May your heart become a tabernacle for His glory-presence, as you pursue His fire in the desert.

Fire in the Desert

The desert and the parched land will be glad; the wilderness will rejoice and blossom. Like the crocus, it will burst into bloom; it will rejoice greatly and shout for joy. The glory of Lebanon will be given to it, the splendour of Carmel and Sharon; they will see the Glory of the Lord, the splendour of our God.

Then will the eyes of the blind be opened and the ears of the deaf unstopped. Then will the lame leap like a deer, and the mute tongue shout for joy.

Water will gush forth in the wilderness and streams in the desert. The burning sand will become a pool, the thirsty grounds bubbling springs.

And a highway will be there; it will be called the Way of Holiness. The unclean will not journey on it; it will be for those who walk in that Way.

Isaiah 35: 1-8

Fire in the Desert

1

Deeper Still

Blessed is the man who trusts in the Lord. He will be like a tree planted by the water that sends out its roots by the stream. It has no worries in a year of drought & never fails to bear fruit

Jeremiah 17:7-8

All around looked dry and barren with dust blowing on the parched land in this sun-scorched nation. The only way to get clean water was to dig deep below the dry, cracked ground. This was the dry season in South Sudan, yet interestingly, it felt like being in a spiritual desert. The only way you could survive in this spiritually dry climate was to go deeper with God, by drinking from His wells of living waters.

As I was trying to survive this hot and arid season, something caught my eye. I noticed there were mango trees all over the land and they were bearing fruit. I wondered how this was possible since we had had no rain for months. Then I discovered the secret. The key was not relying on the showers from above, but on the hidden waters from deep below. The fresh water was being accessed from the roots as they reached deep into the ground.

This made me think how we may rely on the 'showers' or 'blessings' from God to quench our thirst, but struggle when they stop coming. However, it may be a time when we discover how to go deeper in Him, and access His source of living waters from deep below. As we discover the ways to access His living waters, then we will continue to bear fruit whatever season we are in. The Lord said:

"Cursed is the one who trusts in man, who depends on flesh for his strength and whose heart turns away from the Lord. He will be like a bush in the wastelands; he will not see prosperity when it comes. He will dwell in the parched places of the desert, in a salt land where no-one lives. ***But blessed is the man who trusts in the Lord, whose confidence is in Him. He will be like a tree planted by the water that sends out its roots by the stream. It does not fear when heat comes; its leaves are always green. It has no worries in a year of drought and never fails to bear fruit*** *"* (Jeremiah 17:5-8).

The Lord is inviting us to go deeper in Him so we may access His living waters in any drought or crisis situation. A plant with shallow roots will usually struggle to survive during the dry seasons. However, our Father wants us to depend on Him, so we may bear fruit whatever season we may encounter. Our roots grow as we continue to put our faith and trust in Him, instead of trusting in man or our own abilities. The more we lean on Him instead of our own understanding, the deeper our roots will grow.

'Trust in the Lord with all your heart and do not rely on your own understanding; in all your ways acknowledge Him and He will make your paths straight' (Proverb 3:5).

The Israelites struggled across the deserts because they lacked faith and trust in God. They complained and looked elsewhere for their needs, instead of turning to Him. Hence, the first group died in the desert except Joshua and Caleb who put their faith and trust in Him. So God called Joshua to lead the next generation out of the desert and into the Promised Land.

However, the same problem arose again after the Israelites had settled in the Promised Land. His 'bride' had followed Him through the desert, as she depended on Him for her food and protection. However, this was short-lived when she discovered 'alternative resources' in the Promised Land.

*'I remember the **devotion of your youth, how as a bride you loved me and followed me through the desert,** through a land not sown. ...What fault did your fathers find in Me that they strayed so far from Me? **They did not ask,** "Where is the Lord, who brought us up out of Egypt and led us through the barren wilderness, through a land of deserts and rifts, a land of drought and darkness, a land where no-one travels and no-one lives?"....My people have committed two sins: **They have forsaken Me, the Spring of living water, and have dug their own cisterns, broken cisterns that can't hold water'*** (Jeremiah 2:2-3, 6, 13).

Spiritual Wells

God was grieved when His bride became distracted by other things, because she took her eyes off Him and looked for her 'sources' elsewhere. She created 'worldly' cisterns to contain non-flowing water, instead of turning to God for His continuous flow of life-giving water. Worldly cisterns can refer to our wealth and success, or security in finances, ministry, or people, instead of our dependence on God. God is our only source of life-giving water and His supply is unlimited because it never ends. We thirst when we do not look to God for our source, simply because alternative sources fail to produce His life-giving water.

A cistern is usually designed to store or hold water. Hence, the water is non-flowing and may even become stagnant. Also, since it has a limited storage capacity then it may easily run out. However, a well is designed to access fresh flowing water from a source beneath the ground. The source of water usually comes from a river, spring, or ocean, hence it is constantly flowing and there is no end.

Our inner being is like a spiritual well. Some inner wells may need cleansing or unblocking from 'ungodly deposits' that have built up over the years. As God unblocks and removes the ungodly deposits inside our hearts, then His Spirit can reach deeper within. The deeper we go, as we hunger and press into His Spirit, the more His living waters can flow through us and out to others.

Sometimes, God holds back His showers or blessings, to encourage us to seek His source of living waters. He is inviting us to seek Him for our heavenly manna. If God provided fresh manna each day in the desert for the Israelites, how much more will He bend down to feed those who ask?

Jesus said: *'Ask and it shall be given to you; seek and you will find; knock and the door will be opened to you,'* (Matthew 7:7). In the original translation it says, ask and keep on asking, seek and keep on seeking, knock and keep on knocking. And when we persist, God always responds.

Cacti are interesting plants because they know how to survive in the desert. I was given an *Aloe Vera* cactus and soon discovered that when you plant a fresh shoot in soil, you're not meant to give it water for four days. Unlike other plants, the soil must be dry because when the soil is dry then the roots are stimulated to grow.

These plants are designed by God to produce roots in conditions of drought. So where there is drought or thirst, the roots are stimulated to grow deeper, until they find water. This is such a spiritual parallel to growing deeper in the Spirit! Hence, when we start to feel dry or thirsty, He is inviting us to come deeper in Him, to access His living waters.

How Do We Grow Deeper?

God loves to pour out His Spirit as we *pursue Him*. A friend once had a picture of God hiding from me. It was a bit like the game 'hide and seek'. If we want more of His presence, then we are simply to pursue Him. When we seek Him then we will find Him, when we seek Him with all our heart (Jeremiah 29:13).

'It is the glory of God to conceal a matter; to search out a matter is the glory of kings' (Proverbs 25:2). God hides things for us to seek and discover, and hence shares His glory with those who seek and pursue His presence.

Here are some ways we can access His living waters during the spiritually dry seasons.

Hunger for More of Him

One of the ways to go deeper is to hunger in our hearts for more of His presence. God longs to reveal more of Himself, but not through complacency, passivity or compromise. He wants us to pursue Him and find Him. If we lack hunger, then as Heidi baker says, we can ask God to increase our spiritual appetite for more of Him. We mustn't give up thinking God isn't bothered or what is the point, but continue to seek His face during adversities or difficulties.

David constantly sought the presence of God (Psalm 127). Nothing less would satisfy his appetite. He hungered for His presence and waited on the Lord until He showed up. *'Be still before the Lord and wait patiently for Him'* (Psalm 37:7). Are we willing to wait on Him until He shows up? Jesus said: *'Blessed are those who hunger and thirst for righteousness, for they will be filled'* (Matthew 5:6).

There may come a time for us to put aside our own needs or agendas, so we may simply focus on God. When He sees our hungry hearts He will fill us, for it is His desire to draw everyone into a place of deeper communion with Him.

Lord, increase my hunger for You. Thank you there is always more, and You delight in feeding those who hunger and thirst for Your presence.

Prayer and Fasting

Sometimes, when I feel I'm in a spiritual desert, I turn to prayer and fasting. I have discovered that fasting is like a power tool. Fasting remains a mystery but as our flesh yields to our spirit, then our spirit becomes finer tuned to hearing God. God responds when He sees we are desperate for His presence. When He sees our yielded, desperate hearts, then out of His awesome love He responds.

Fasting is like a power drill that breaks through dry ground. The enemy will tempt us with all reasons why we shouldn't fast, for he knows the power of fasting. However, Jesus fasted in the desert during His forty days of spiritual opposition and breakthrough.

Fasting is one of the most powerful spiritual weapons we have. Satanists regularly fast to upgrade their demonic power when coming against God's people. How much more then should we fast when engaging in battles or seeking breakthrough? There are different ways to fast and this is beyond the scope of this book, but I encourage you to read more on this subject.[1] [2]

During a season of transition, I somehow felt stuck not knowing where I was going and started to doubt if God was with me. Because I felt so lost and desperate in my spirit, I went on a fast. I was desperate for His presence and to know His will in my life. Then on the third day of the fast, there was breakthrough. Suddenly, His loving presence crashed down on me as He saw my heart crying out to Him. As I felt His presence so tangibly in and around me, I knew I had nothing to fear. My heart was once more at peace as I discovered His will and realised this was a significant season He had set up for me. He revealed this 'wilderness' season was an important time of spiritual preparation, and unless I yielded to His Spirit and counsel, I wouldn't be ready to step into what He had next. Breakthrough was achieved through fasting, and this enabled me to go deeper as I yielded to Him.

Jesus fasted so His Spirit could overcome the battles in the wilderness. Fasting enables us to hear and see more clearly in the Spirit, as we surrender our flesh to God. Though fasting may not seem easy, it helps to overcome our flesh and fine tunes our spirit to the sensitivity of God's Spirit. Fasting is a valuable tool, especially when seeking direction, breakthrough, and for overcoming our spiritual battles.

Jesus told His disciples not *if* but *when* they fast (Matthew 5:16). When the Bridegroom was taken from them, then they would fast (Matthew 9:15). Fasting is a spiritual weapon that draws us closer to God. Remember, the enemy tempts us with all reasons and lies, why we shouldn't fast and how trivial it is, for he doesn't want us to know the true power behind fasting. If Jesus needed to fast to overcome the enemy and make it through the desert, then perhaps we do too.

Lord Jesus, give me Your grace to fast. Show me when, how long and what type of fast to do. Teach me the power behind fasting, and help me to press deeper in You. Thank you, that prayer and fasting releases breakthrough.

Feed on His Word

Another way to go deeper is by feeding on His living word. There are different levels of revelation that are hidden in the word of God, and He reveals these pearls of wisdom to His children.

Reading over the same scriptures can be a bit like digging deeper over the same patch of ground. What we discover initially will be different to what we discover when we dig deeper over the same area. One of the temptations we may face when we feel spiritually dry is to stop reading His word. We may start to think it is no help anymore or we have already read it and don't need to read it again. The opposite is true, for this is a time when we are to ask God to increase our spiritual appetite and feed us with fresh manna from His word.

Sometimes, God may give us fresh insight into well known passages of scripture, as if we are reading with a new pair of lenses. This is when He gives us a deeper level of understanding through fresh revelation and divine insight. There are various levels of revelation that can be discovered in the same passages of scripture.

Hence, His word is sharp and living like a two edge sword, and increases the fire in our hearts (Hebrew 4:12). When Jesus spoke to the two men on the road to Emmaus, His living Word burned in their hearts as He revealed the scriptures to them from a different perspective. *'Were not our hearts burning within us while He talked with us on the road and opened the Scriptures to us?'* (Luke 24:32).

God provided fresh manna each day for His people during their time in the wilderness. Likewise, He will give us fresh manna, that is, fresh revelation from His word, if we seek Him and ask.

Lord Jesus, may Your Word be living and active, like a two-edged sword burning right through my heart. May it carry words of revelation, truth and life, as I eagerly seek Your face.

Praying In the Spirit.

One of the ways to tune into the Spirit is with a supernatural prayer language. The gift of tongues is a prayer language that is given to every Spirit-filled believer by the Holy Spirit. I believe it is a gift for everyone since it helps our spirit to engage with God's Spirit. It helps us to connect to the Holy Spirit and pray more effectively in the Spirit. When we pray in tongues we are in effect interceding in the Spirit, and the Spirit knows how we ought to pray in every given situation.

'In the same way the Spirit helps us in our weakness. We do not know what we ought to pray for, but the Spirit Himself intercedes for us with groans that words can't express' (Romans 8:26).

We are encouraged to *pray in the Spirit* on all occasions (Ephesians 6:18). We can ask God for a prayer language, then by faith receive it and start to speak it. The more we use it on a regular basis, the more words will start to flow. It is not about understanding what we say, but igniting our spirit with the Holy Spirit through this gift. It can be a bit like the fuel in a plane needed for takeoff. Praying in tongues helps us to move from earthly mindsets to Kingdom mindsets, as we connect our spirit with His.

'For if I pray in a tongue, my spirit prays, but my mind is unfruitful. So what shall I do? I will pray with my spirit, but I will also pray with my mind; I will sing with my spirit but I will also sing with my mind,' (1 Corinthians 14:14).

I have found this useful in my own prayer life but also when interceding or praying for others. When I pray in my spiritual language, sometimes the Holy Spirit takes over and I sense the power of God's Spirit moving in the situation.

Contemporary prophets encourage us to pray in tongues for at least an hour every day. As we pray in the Spirit, our minds and spirits become more sharpened and sensitive to God's Spirit.

Recently, a pastor preached on the gift of tongues then invited the church to pray in tongues with him, for half an hour each morning. The fruit from this was amazing. People not only discovered how to pray in tongues on a daily basis, but their spirit became more sensitive to hear and sense the Spirit of God.

Whenever we pray in the Spirit it builds up our faith (Jude 1:20). I find it useful to pray in my prayer language when worshiping or out walking or driving, as well as when praying with others. It is an amazing weapon for breakthrough. I have found it especially effective when coming against any spirit of apathy, oppression, or demonic stronghold.

Whenever I struggle to give thanks and praise, I default to praying in tongues. I somehow find this easier since it helps me overcome spiritual opposition, as my spirit directly engages with God's Spirit. The gift of praying in tongues enables us to pray in the Spirit, especially when we are struggling to pray in our native language.

To my surprise, I discovered from a pastor that it is possible to pray in tongues silently or without uttering words from our mouth. This is praying in tongues in our spirit but without speaking aloud. The benefit of this is that it is non-threatening to those around us and means we can pray in the Spirit continually.

Lord, teach me how to pray in the Spirit. Thank you for the gift of tongues and how it is a tool for breakthrough, intercession and to help me engage with Your Spirit. Lord, I ask for this gift, and by faith I receive it. Teach me Holy Spirit, how to pray in the Spirit and be led by Your Spirit. Help me to daily pray in the Spirit with You. Thank you Jesus.

Giving Thanks and Praise

Each time we choose to give Him thanks and praise, our spirit connects with His. Even if we don't feel His presence we can still worship, because Christ dwells in our hearts *by faith* (Ephesians 3:17).

The enemy tries to pull us down with fears, anxieties, burdens, oppression, apathy, hopelessness, despair, worldly temptations, self-centred thoughts, and so on. Instead, we can overcome negative thoughts and feelings, by choosing to give Him thanks and praise. As our spirit engages with His Spirit, it will rise above the negative thoughts we are feeling.

Thanksgiving and praise draws us closer to Him, because we enter His gates *with thanksgiving* and His courts *with praise* (Psalm 100:4). Everything looks different when we start to see things through His eyes and heart. Worldly perception is contrary to the way God sees, for God's thoughts are not our thoughts (Isaiah 55:8). Thanksgiving and praise helps to turn our hearts to Him, and this in turn enables us to discern His ways.

It is not easy to give God thanks and praise, especially when we feel low in spirit. Yet, this is what we are commanded to do, especially when we don't feel like doing it. It is like hitting hard ground and feeling discouraged by what we see, or thinking there is no way through. During such times, we are not to judge by what we naturally see, or hear, or feel, but allow our spiritual eyes to see what God is doing. He knows what is coming before we do and is simply waiting to see our response.

Paul learned to give thanks to God in *all circumstances,* for he knew God would break through for him. When Paul and Silas were beaten and thrown in prison, they didn't moan but instead gave thanks and praise. Shortly after, there was a rumble and the prison doors flew open.

God is the God of the impossible. He is simply testing our hearts when He allows impossible situations to come our way. Paul gave the Thessalonians 'three pills' to take each day: *'Be **joyful always；** **pray continually； give thanks in all circumstances**, for this is God's will for you in Christ Jesus'* (1 Thessalonians 5:16).

Moaning and complaining attract ungodly spirits including self-pity, whereas thanksgiving and praise attract God's ministering angels, and also His Spirit. Thanks and praise provides a way for God to move, where as complaining and judging opens a door for the enemy to move. David learnt how to turn each crisis to God, with thanks and praise, even if it meant waiting for God to act. God was always there for him, even if it wasn't as quickly as he wanted.

Thanksgiving and praise are important warfare tools to align our hearts with God and stay tuned in Him. It not only keeps our hearts at peace but allows God to move in our circumstances. Nothing is too difficult for Him since He can see things coming before we can. How we respond is the key to how we will get through, as we look to God for our solution.

Lord, give me a heart that gives You thanks and praise no matter what my circumstance may be. Help me to see Your hand in the bigger scheme of things, and have faith in You for the impossible.

Confidence in God

Many times my faith and trust in God have been tested, especially when I may start to doubt His word or promises. Whenever I allow fear or anxiety to enter my mind, my inner peace disappears and I start to think He isn't with me or I need to do something. During such times, I have found praying with friends has helped me to re-focus my mind on Him and hold onto His promises.

One of the hardest things to do when in the desert is to put our confidence in God.

The word confidence comes from the French and Latin word *confide* which means to boldly put your 'faith', 'trust 'or 'strength' in something. We have a choice of where we put our confidence - in 'self', 'others' or 'God'.

Self-confidence sounds good but is a form of pride for in effect we are putting out faith and trust in our 'self' or our own abilities. I believe God wants us to put our confidence not in ourselves or others, but in Him alone.

I was walking along the beach one windy day when I saw a man step in the water with a surf board and kite-sail. As his kite caught the wind, he took off surfing on the waves across the ocean. It was spectacular to see the wind carry him across the sea, out of his depth, as he held on with complete confidence, trust and faith. He had no fear of losing his life or being out of his depth. He simply surrendered to the power of the wind as it took him to unreached places. We can have this same confidence in God's Spirit as we daily surrender to the move and power of His Spirit in us. As we hold on to God's words and His promises, they will strengthen our faith in times of need.

Lord, help me to put my confidence not in myself, but in Your Word and Your Spirit.

Leave the Old Self Behind

Sometimes, the Spirit takes us through the desert so we may leave our 'old self' behind. Our old self includes the ways of our carnal nature and flesh. Jesus had to die to His flesh in order for His Spirit to overcome the tests and trials in the desert.

'Put to death, therefore, whatever belongs to your earthly nature: sexual immorality, impurity, lust, evil desires and greed, that is idolatry...do not lie to each other, since you have taken off your old self with its practices and have put on the new self, which is being renewed in knowledge in the image of its Creator' (Colossians 3:5-10).

The biggest temptation in the desert is to give up on God and focus on self, or the ways of the world. The enemy will try every tactic to tempt us to give up on following God. Our first battle ground is the battle of our mind. The enemy subtly tempts us with thoughts about self, so we end up putting our self or flesh first. This may cause us to fall away from God whilst in the desert.

Focusing on self is the root of pride, and pride made Satan fall from God's Kingdom (Ezekiel 28:17, Isaiah 14:13-14). One of the ways to overcome the enemy's subtle temptations is to take captive our thoughts and make them obedient to Christ (2 Corinthians 10:4-5). The desert is the perfect place where we learn to die to our flesh and self.

Lord, reveal the areas and attitudes of my mind that I'm to yield to You. Show me how to grow more in Your ways and renew my mind, so my thoughts may be pleasing to You.

Deep Calling unto Deep

In Ezekiel, we read about the river of Life flowing through God's temple. When the river had flowed across roughly half a kilometre, it was only ankle deep. It took a further half a kilometre before it became knee deep. And another half a kilometre before it became waist deep. And another half a kilometre before the river was flowing above the heads. It took time and perseverance to wade across to the deeper levels in the river. In other words, to go deeper in Him means spending time seeking Him and abiding or *soaking* in His presence, as we choose to pursue Him.

The Lord spoke to me in a vision of the ocean, where the ocean represented God's presence and the shore represented the world. I saw a mist hovering over the shallow waters of the shore. This mist represented spiritual deception. The people on the shore seemed engrossed in worldly affairs and fed from the tree of Knowledge of Good and Evil. However, some were standing ankle deep in the ocean, gaining momentary insight into the Kingdom, but still listening to man's ideas, opinions or things of the world. They hadn't fully surrendered their ambition, control, fear, or doubt, and this prevented them going deeper. Then there were those who waded in the water and fully immersed themselves in the ocean of His presence. They humbled themselves as they dived below the mist of deception, in total abandonment to His Spirit. The further they went in the depths of the ocean, the clearer they could see as they left the mist behind. Then I heard the words, 'Deep calls unto deep' (Psalm 42:7).

The Lord is calling us to a deeper place of intimacy with Him, as we abandon ourselves in the ocean of His presence. It is leaving all man-made ideas, man-made theologies, agendas and worldly strategies behind, as we seek His face in the depths of His presence. This is the place of surrender and abandonment as we pursue Him. It is in this place of surrender and abandonment, where we receive His wisdom and revelation, along with Kingdom strategies, both for the present and future.

Jesus spent most of His life, thirty years, preparing for His three and a half years of ministry. He patiently waited for the right time before He did His first miracle. He knew this moment would change everything. Hence, when Mary asked Him to turn the water into wine, He said His timing had not yet come (John 2:4). He humbly waited for the right time before He came out of 'hiding' in the secret place with God.

During these thirty years, He had an intimate relationship with His Father as He lived in complete obedience to His Father's will. He simply rested in His Father's presence. He performed miracles and healing, not to glorify Himself, but to glorify His Father and to reveal His Father's love to His people. All He did came from an intimate relationship of Sonship with the Father. He knew His Father would give Him what He asked, because He walked in such intimacy with Him. This is the same intimacy the Father is inviting you and me to have with Him, as deep calls unto deep.

Lord, forgive me for when I focus on myself and my problems instead of focusing on You. Forgive me for when I make wrong choices and go down wrong paths. Lord, I want to be with You, on Your path of Life. Help me to hear You and know Your ways. Lord, I need You, I am desperate for You. Increase my hunger for more of Your presence.

ENDNOTES

[1] Mahesh Chavda; *The Hidden Power of Prayer and Fasting,* (Destiny Image 1998).

[2] Angela Walker; *Kingdom Medicine Volume 1: Foundation For Healing,* chapt 12 (2020)

2

Metamorphosis

Be transformed by the renewing of your mind

Romans 12:2

The word *metamorphosis* comes from the Greek word, *'metamorphoo'*[1] and means to be *'transformed'*. According to the Oxford English Dictionary, the word 'metamorphosis' can mean three things;

   I. *To change form by natural or supernatural means*
  II. *A change of character*
 III. *The transformation from immature to adult form*

Three times this word is used in the New Testament and we find that the above meanings are implied in each text.

First, the word was used when Jesus was 'transfigured' on the mountain. *'There He was **transfigured [metamorphoo]** before them. His face shone like the sun and His clothes became as white as the light'* (Matthew 17:2). Here is the first definition, where Jesus was being transformed from *natural to supernatural*.

The same word is used when Paul teaches on being 'transformed' by the renewing of our minds.

'*Do not conform any more to the pattern of this world but be transformed [metamorphoo] by the renewing of your mind*' (Romans 12:2). This is referring to a *change in our mindset and character,* as we see in the second definition.

Likewise, Paul used the same word when he spoke to the Corinthians. '*And we, who with unveiled faces all reflect the Lord's glory,* **are being transformed [metamorphoo] into His likeness with ever increasing glory**' (2 Corinthians 3:18). Here, the word is used to describe the process of *maturing in our spirit,* as we see in the third definition.

From Caterpillar to Butterfly

The best natural and well known example of metamorphosis is when a caterpillar is radically transformed into a butterfly. This is a very interesting process that is worth mentioning in more detail.

Natural Process

The life cycle of a butterfly starts when an egg is laid by the adult butterfly. This multiplies and gradually takes the form of a caterpillar. The caterpillar has to moult its skin or shell in order to increase in size. The role of a caterpillar is simply to feed and grow. However, when it reaches a certain size it produces a cocoon as it gets ready to hibernate. It then takes the form of a chrysalis as it lies dormant on the inside of the cocoon. On the outside it appears to be doing nothing, but this is far from the truth, for on the inside it is undergoing what is known as 'auto-digestion'. During this process of auto-digestion, it is secreting enzymes to digest its 'self'. As the chrysalis is being digested by these enzymes, it forms a protein-rich liquid that becomes the source of food for the next phase of its growth.

All that is left behind, unaffected by the auto-digestion process, are what are known as *imaginal discs*. These are in effect, stem cells and contain the genetic material, or DNA, that is required to create the butterfly. Multiplication of the stem cells begins as they feed from this protein-rich liquid.

The stem cells continue to multiply until they produce the form of a butterfly. The butterfly continues to grow in size until it is ready to break out of the cocoon. The butterfly not only looks totally different but has a different function to the caterpillar. It is lighter, more colourful and is no more earth-bound, but air-borne. The butterfly no longer has to stay in the same place like the caterpillar, but can cross-pollinate and fly all over to different places on the thermal currents in the air.

Supernatural Transformation

The whole process of being transformed from a caterpillar to a butterfly is like our spiritual growth. Like the caterpillar, we begin to grow by feeding on God's word and Spirit. As we continue to grow, we may find ourselves reaching certain phases in our spiritual development where we are somehow required to break through in order to enter the next stage in our journey with God. This is like the shedding of the outer shell of the caterpillar, that takes us to the floor or beginning of the next phase in our spiritual growth. This shift from one level to the next usually involves some degree of spiritual breakthrough. This is because we may need to break out of the old way before we can step into the new way. It is like having growth spurts in the different phases of our spiritual nurturing.

However, after several layers have been shed, we reach a point in our spiritual growth where we come to the phase of the chrysalis. This may seem strange since we have spent the past years growing in order to arrive at the next phase which is one of death or death-to-self. This is because it is a time of death to our flesh or carnal nature which is an important process in the transformation of our inner being. For many, this will seem like journeying through the wilderness and encountering the cross. For others, it may be a time of 'spiritual rest'.

When we reach a certain phase in our spiritual growth, Jesus may invite us to embrace the cross. This is when He personally invites us to lay down our lives for Him. On the outside it may seem we are doing nothing, yet on the inside we are undergoing transformation in our hearts and minds.

A pastor gave me a picture that described the chrysalis season in my life. She had a picture of a room with closed curtains where the room was being renovated. Hence, those on the outside couldn't see what was going on the inside until the room was finished. When the curtains were opened, the room looked transformed and radically different to before.

After serving for some years in Africa, the Lord led me through a season of transition. God revealed this was a season of 'spiritual rest,' where I was to stop what I was doing and rest in Him. He was revealing the secret to abiding in His presence. However, during this season of spiritual rest I was also undergoing a process of inner transformation. At the beginning, He revealed that I was entering the *'chrysalis'* phase. This was confirmed by others, along with the words *'hemmed in'*. God explained that He was drawing me aside from the things of the world, so He could do a deeper work in my heart.

David knew what it meant to be hemmed in by the Lord. '*You **hem me in**- behind and before;* ***You have laid Your hand upon me***' (Psalm 139:5).

I struggled with this season, for I wanted to be back on the mission field, reaping in the harvest and serving Him in Africa. To others it looked like I was doing nothing but wasting time.

However, this 'chrysalis' phase was an important season of dying to my flesh, as I entered the 'auto-digestive' phase. It was a season for God to crucify different areas of my 'self', so my carnal nature no longer ruled, but rather His Spirit reigned instead. During this time, He brought to my attention the different areas of my heart I was to put on the altar and surrender to Him. For most of the time, this was neither easy nor pleasant, and felt quite painful in the process. However, the process was well worth enduring in order to experience the freedom and joy that lay ahead.

As sons and daughters of God, we are invited to embrace pain, rather than run from it. Jesus had to embrace pain when He faced the cross. However, He did this fully knowing the joy that was set before Him (Hebrews 12:2). Where there is a death, there is also a resurrection. For everything we die to in our flesh, God will transform it into something beautiful in the Spirit. I believe the people I know who carry the most beautiful, radiant, and transparent vessels, are those who have undergone the greatest auto-digestion or death-to-self.

Kingdom DNA

Once the auto-digestion is complete, the stem cells, that represent the Kingdom DNA, can come into operation. As we allow His Spirit to transform our hearts, He will gradually renew our hearts and minds, so we take on His character and attitude. However, this is a continual and ongoing process.

Paul said: *'Be transformed by the renewing of your minds'* (Romans 12:2). This isn't a one off experience, but an ongoing renewal. It is a constant process of inward 'renewing' or 'rewiring' of our thought patterns. When we are born again, we have simply become newborn babies in His Kingdom. Spiritual growth takes place as we constantly feed on His word and Spirit. Transformation is part of our spiritual nurturing and occurs as we yield each part of our heart and self to Him.

One of the key areas in this process of inner transformation is resting in His presence. The chrysalis has to rest or cease work. God can perform deeper work in our hearts during these seasons of spiritual rest. It is like being on an operating table, where we have to be still in His presence. And as we rest in Him, we discover the ways of His heart. The Psalmist said: *'Be still and know that I am God'* (Psalm 46:10). This is referring to us *experientially* knowing Him in our hearts. God can do deep work in our hearts as we chose to rest or soak in His presence. This yielding is like giving Him consent to minister to our hearts.

Jesus had to wait until He was thirty before He entered His ministry. He was led through the wilderness for an intense forty days of trials and tests. After overcoming every test and trial, by yielding His flesh to the Spirit of God, He received a fresh outpouring and anointing, to step into His three and a half years of ministry.

Pumping of Wings

After I had entered the 'chrysalis' phase, it took a further two years before I felt I was coming into the 'butterfly' phase. This was confirmed by a friend who saw me in the Spirit, like a butterfly with outstretched wings. However, I was in the 'drying wings' phase. I still had to be patient as God was doing the finer, more intricate work to the design in the wings. I had a picture of having outstretched wings needing to be pumped with blood. As I saw them being pumped up with blood, they expanded and increased, becoming two to three times in size. Their weight became lighter in the process.

After receiving this vision, I decided to find out what happens in the natural when the butterfly breaks out of the shell. Apparently, as the butterfly breaks forth out of the cocoon, its wings become pumped with blood and expand up to three times in size. The wings are then held out to dry, before it eventually flies off.

Naturally, it only takes a few hours for a butterfly to pump up and dry the wings. However, spiritually, this process takes much longer. Spiritually speaking, the pumping of blood and expansion of wings may be gradual or immediate. On one hand, it may be likened to a fresh impartation or anointing of the Spirit being released to us. On the other hand, this process of pumping with blood and expansion of wings may be a more gradual phase. As the blood slowly passes through the wings, it may perform the final cleansing and refining. This causes the wings to increase in size, and this can be likened to His Spirit expanding in us. This is like developing an increase in the capacity of our hearts to host His presence, as we allow Him to crucify the areas of our 'self' or flesh.

The 'drying' phase of the wings, can also be a time of waiting and resting in the Lord, as He tests the 'new' areas in our hearts.

After this process of inner transformation, a new being emerges that can engage in a deeper place of intimacy with Him, as a result of resting in His presence. As transformed beings, God can send us out to cross-pollinate in the world, in different places, people groups, and nations, as we learn to effortlessly move on the wind of His Spirit.

Corporate Transformation

I happened to be in a meeting concerning the plans for a new church building, when the leaders commented that the outer body work of the building was to remain untouched, whereas the inner body work was to undergo complete demolition and reconstruction. This was interesting because it reminded me of the chrysalis phase of the butterfly, and the words 'corporate transformation' immediately sprung to mind. A few days later, during a time of corporate worship, a young girl had a prophetic picture of a caterpillar becoming a butterfly. I then realised God was confirming 'corporate transformation' in the body of Christ. Paul referred to this when he said:

'In Him the whole building is joined together and rises to become a holy temple in the Lord. And in Him you (plural) too are being built together to become a dwelling in which God lives by His Spirit' (Ephesians 2:22).

It was interesting what transpired during the outbreak of the Corona Virus, *Covid 19,* in 2020. Most nations went into lockdown to apparently prevent the spread of the virus and reduce the death rate. As a result of this, people were instructed to stay in their homes and if possible, to work from home. Also, children were home-schooled, and the churches started to provide 'on-line' services. Nearly everything was taking place in the home and through the internet or social media. I suddenly saw how this could be an opportunity for corporate transformation to occur in families and churches, as people withdrew from the outside world to retreat in their 'homes' or their 'inner dwelling places'.

Some prophets saw the lockdown as an opportunity for coming into the ark of His presence, in the same way Noah retreated in the ark during the flood. It is interesting that the rains were for forty days and nights, but the flood lasted around ten and a half months.

Many of us may still be functioning as caterpillars instead of butterflies. Some may disagree, but I believe the gifts of the Spirit mentioned in 1 Corinthians 12 are for the caterpillar phase of growth. This is because they are freely given when we are born-again and filled with the Spirit, hence, they do not reflect spiritual maturity. They are given by the Holy Spirit to encourage and nurture us in our spiritual growth (Hebrews 6:1-3).

However, the chrysalis phase is a season of transition where our hearts undergo an inner transformation. It is a costly season, for it involves dying to our carnal nature and this involves encountering the cross. A well known prophet commented that the way of transformation is a cross-shaped life. It is through the grace of God that we can encounter the cross, and this is different for each one of us. The Lord may show some of us when we have reached the butterfly stage of maturity, for His Spirit will bring this revelation to our hearts. After all, it is the Spirit who testifies with our spirit that we are God's children (Romans 8:16).

Whereas the caterpillar stays on the ground chewing away and increasing in size, the butterfly is designed to fly to other places and cross-pollinate. The butterfly represents a life in the Spirit, where we go where the Spirit leads and do what we see Him doing. This is *effortless* ministry because we have learnt to operate no longer by might, nor by strength, but by the power of His Spirit (Zechariah 4:6).

After the disciples corporately waited on the Lord, spending time in His presence, suddenly everything changed. In God's perfect timing, they received their anointing directly from the Holy Spirit. They were now to go and disciple the *nations* by spreading His word and 'cross-pollinating', as they reached out to distant people groups. They were transformed from caterpillars to butterflies. Instead of functioning from their flesh, they were now operating under the power and anointing of His Spirit.

It is interesting that the Jewish festivals Passover and Pentecost for 2020 were celebrated in the homes due to the *Covid 19* lockdown. Some believe this was the Passover of all Passovers, as the *plague of death* 'passed over' our nations. Also, it was a season of incubation and preparation, as we waited on God for the fresh anointing or outpouring of His Spirit.

Just as God prepared the hearts of His disciples for the outpouring at Pentecost, so I believe He is preparing our hearts to get ready for the new waves or moves of His Spirit.

Fire in the Desert

Lord Jesus, I give You permission to circumcise every part of my heart. I no longer want my old self or carnal nature to live, but invite You to transform my inner being, through Your Word and Spirit. Teach me how to live a naturally supernatural life as I daily surrender my flesh to You. Transform every part in me, so it is no longer I who live but You who lives in me.

END NOTES

[1] Metamorphoo (Greek 3339); *Strong's Expanded Exhaustive Concordance: Red Letter Edition*

3

His Resting Place

Where will My resting place be?

Acts 7:49

After finishing a mission assignment in South Sudan, I realised I was entering a season of transition. Initially, I thought this meant a change of nations, until I later realised God was calling me to a change of lifestyle. This was not meant to be a short-term assignment, because He was calling me to a lifestyle of abiding in His presence.

I soon discovered that abiding in His presence seemed more important to Him than the work I did for Him. He was inviting me to His resting place. He made it clear that I was no longer to focus on my work or ministry or even be concerned with what I did next. He just wanted me to focus on Him and daily come into His presence. Whenever I tried to get back into mission work, the doors seemed to be shut. On questioning God why this was happening, He said it simply wasn't His will or timing, and that's why He hadn't allowed the doors to open.

Transition

When the Lord gave me the word 'transition', I felt a peace, though I wasn't quite sure what He meant. During this season, I found myself in a huge battle. This was because my flesh was at war with my spirit. My flesh was arguing, *'You should be doing something for you have much to offer. Don't waste your time,'* but my spirit said, *'Rest in the Lord. Your life is now in His hands. You belong to Him.'*

Then I was given a prophetic word from someone who didn't know me. In this prophetic word, I was resisting God by trying to get back on the mission field, to do the work He had previously called me to. Yet God was lovingly holding me, and asking me to simply yield everything to Him. He was wooing me into His place of rest and into a deeper union with Him. He wanted me to reach a place in my spirit where I could be completely one with Him, in perfect union with His Spirit; I in Him and Him in me (John 14:20).

The reason I had struggled with this was because there were areas in my flesh that were still resisting or fighting back. I realised these were the carnal areas that He wanted me to yield to Him. This became easier once I realised that my relationship with Him mattered more than what I did for Him.

When we enter a season of transition, it may mean we have to let go of the old order of doing things in order to enter the new. This is like closing one door behind us, then having to walk across a bridge or through a tunnel, until we reach the new door on the other side. For some, God may be pressing a pause button, and for others, He may be leading them into a new era or chapter with Him. However, it's during the crossing over phase that we mustn't be tempted to give up or turn back. We must be careful not to let the fear of the unknown hold us back, but keep moving forward in faith and obedience to His Spirit.

The most important thing during a season of transition is that we respond to whatever God wants to do in our hearts. Hence, our response will determine our outcome.

Assigned Rest

Over the next two years, I kept receiving the same word: 'REST'. Even at a mission's conference, I received the word, 'Assigned Rest.' I was so used to God sending me out on missions, but never to go on an 'assignment of rest'. Who would have thought that rest could be an assignment from God?

During this time of rest, I wasn't to engage in any ministry or work, but use it for seeking God and going deeper in Him. It was a time to let Him change my old patterns of thinking and become more *self-aware*, as He revealed my strengths but also my character flaws and weaknesses. In this rest, He wanted to reveal more of Himself, His ways and how He sees me. He was stripping me of my old clothes in order to take on His new royal garments (Zechariah 3).

This was a slow process as He dealt with each issue in turn. I kept thinking it was over after He dealt with one issue, until He would reveal the next and the next. He was taking me to a place of no longer caring about what I did next, but simply enjoying my time being with Him, abiding in His loving presence.

God's deepest desire is to find a resting place in our hearts, where He may come and tabernacle with us. We know that our body needs rest when we feel tired and exhausted, but spiritual rest is different. To rest in the Lord means to engage in His presence. Each time our inner spirit engages with God, we go deeper in our relationship with Him. This is not passive but rather active, as we turn our hearts to Him.

Sabbath Rest

The Hebrew word for Sabbath is taken from the verb *Shabbat*, [1] and means 'to rest'. Sabbath is a time for rest. This verb is first seen in the Book of Genesis chapter 2:2-3: *'So on the seventh day He **rested** from all His work. And God blessed the seventh day and made it holy, because on it He **rested** from all the work of creating what He had done.'*

When He spoke to Moses, He said: *'Six days do your work, but on the seventh day do not work'* (Exodus 23:12). Man would cease from his work in order to rest and spend time with God. The Lord made Sabbath for man, not man for the Sabbath. Jesus said: *'The Son of Man is Lord of the Sabbath'* (Luke 6:5). Since God made the Sabbath, then He is Lord of the Sabbath. After all, the Sabbath is all about entering a place of rest with Him.

There is the weekly day of rest, known as the *Sabbath day*, but also longer periods of rest, known as *Sabbaticals*. Sabbaticals may last for a period of months or even a year. It was the Jewish custom to take a *year of Sabbath* rest every six years. This was usually a year of rest from work.

*'When you enter the land I am going to give you, the land itself must observe a Sabbath to the Lord. For six years, sow your fields, and for six years prune your vineyards and gather their crops. **But in the seventh year the land is to have a Sabbath of rest, a Sabbath to the Lord**. Do not sow your fields or prune your vineyards. Do not reap what grows of itself or harvest the grapes of your unattended vines. The land is to **have a year of rest**. Whatever the land yields during the Sabbath year will be food for you'* (Leviticus 25:1-7).

After this, there was another year of Sabbath taken every forty nine years. The Lord commanded Moses to count off seven Sabbaths of years. This is seven times seven or forty nine years. On the Day of Atonement or *Yom Kippur*, they would sound the trumpet and declare the beginning of the fiftieth year. The beginning of the fiftieth year is known as the *Year of Jubilee*, a time of liberty throughout the land for all of the people (Leviticus 25: 8-24).

A sabbatical is meant to be a specific time to cease all work. Some take a sabbatical to simply have a time of rest, whereas others use the time to go deeper in their fellowship with God.

There came a time shortly after I became a Paediatric Consultant, when I felt a stirring in my spirit to take a two month sabbatical. However, little did I know that the two months would end up being a five month sabbatical.

The first month was full of expectations as I began spending each morning with God in my garden. This was a beautiful time as I felt His presence waiting for me each morning. However, this changed once I entered the beginning of the second month. Suddenly, I no longer sensed His presence waiting for me. Instead, I felt alone, as if I had entered a desert. It felt as if He had withdrawn His presence. Then I realised I was entering a 'spiritual desert' in my journey with Him, and this time was as important as the first month in the 'spiritual garden'.

Each month of the sabbatical was different as God was doing deeper things in my heart and asking me to lay down things for Him. At the end, He was leading me down a completely different path that was going to change my life and career.

I discovered that the Lord is with us in the different spiritual seasons of our life, whether in the desert, on the mountain top, in the garden, or in the valleys. His presence is the same throughout. It is just that we sense more of His presence when we are on top of the mountain or all is going well, compared to the barren seasons or when feeling alone. It is important we hang in there, and let God complete in us what He has started, knowing He is always with us. Hence, it is important we do not give up, but stick at God's plans and purposes during the desert seasons.

Sabbaticals are life changing if we allow God to be in charge and surrender our hearts to Him. The Lord said this about His bride: *'I am now going to allure her; I will lead her into the desert and speak tenderly to her'* (Hosea 2:14).

There is another Sabbath rest that goes beyond the ones so far mentioned. This is the *lifestyle* of resting in His presence. It is discovering how to work from a place of spiritual rest. In order to reach this place of rest in Him, God has to do deeper work in our hearts. This includes giving Him our fears, doubts, false beliefs, negative thoughts, as well as handing Him the control reins in our lives. By allowing Him to deal with each area in our hearts, we will reach a deeper place of rest and union in Him. When we have reached this place of divine rest, our circumstances will no longer worry us, because our hearts will be deeply rooted in Him.

Enter His Rest

I believe the Lord is calling us to a lifestyle of divine rest in Him. Jesus rested in His Father, for He only did what He saw His Father do. All His work flowed from a life of abiding in the Spirit. He did nothing in the flesh. He gave all control to His Father for He came to do His Father's will and was always about His Father's business. After He overcame the battles in the wilderness, the Spirit of the Lord came and fully *rested* on Him (Luke 4:18, Isaiah 11:2).

The author of Hebrews revealed there was and still is a resting place of God. On the seventh day God rested from His work and we are invited to enter this same place of rest with Him.

'There remains then, a Sabbath-rest for the people of God; for anyone who enters God's rest, also rests from his own work, just as God did from His' *(Hebrews 4:9-10).*

I believe this is referring to a lifestyle of resting in His Spirit. It is more than a temporary break from work. It is coming to a place of complete union in our hearts with Him.

Many of the End-Time prophets believe we have now entered the season of 'rest'. Peter said a thousand years can be like a day: *'But do not forget this one thing friends; with the Lord a day is like a thousand years and a thousand years like a day,'* (2 Peter 3:8). This implies that since there were four thousand years between Adam and Jesus and two thousand years after Jesus, we are now in the seventh millennium or seventh day. This seventh millennium represents the season of divine rest. Hence, this is a season to no longer strive in our flesh, but rather work from a place of resting in His presence. What we do is no longer to be in our own might or strength, but by the power of His Spirit abiding in us.

I believe we are all called to enter His rest. But what does this mean? One day as I was out cycling in the forest, enjoying the beautiful summer breeze, I sensed God say to my spirit, *'Ange, will you be 24:7 with Me?'* This came as a surprise. Though I said 'yes', I didn't really know what this would entail. Slowly, over the years, I have understood what this means. It is a life of abiding in His presence. This means laying down our own agendas or plans and choosing to be in tune with His Spirit twenty four hours every day of the week.

If we want to enter His rest, then it requires us to no longer strive or slave away by working in our own strength. We can only enter His rest when we choose to yield ourselves to Him. Most of the time, we just have a miniscule taste of His rest. However, there is a much deeper place of rest He wants each of us to enter, and this comes from yielding every part of our life and self to Him.

What Do You Want?

Most of us, if we are honest, pursue God or turn to God when we want something from Him. This is the 'immature' child in us. A little child follows their parent when they want something from them. The moment they have what they want, they may leave their parent and go away, or focus on the things they were given, be it sweets, a toy or something else.

When two of John the Baptist's disciples followed Jesus, He asked them, *'What do you want?'* Instantly, He thought they were pursuing Him to get something. However, they were following Him for one reason – to be with Him. They wanted to know Him and have fellowship with Him. Their eyes were not on the gifts but the Giver Himself.

'The next day John was there with two of his disciples. When he saw Jesus passing by he said, "Look, the Lamb of God!" When the two disciples heard him say this, they followed Jesus. Turning around, Jesus saw them following and asked, **"What do you want?"** *They said, "Rabbi" (which means Teacher),* **"Where are You staying." Jesus replied, "Come, and you will see."** *So they went and saw where He was staying and spent that day with Him'* (John 1: 35-39).

This is profound. These two disciples didn't want to meet Jesus for their own selfish gain or to receive a blessing, but to get to know Him. They wanted to dine and fellowship with Him and become His friends. To do this meant they had to hang out with Him. They wanted to stay with Him. His home became their home.

This same invitation is open to you and me, to come and rest with Jesus, so we may abide in Him and He may abide in us. Jesus is looking for true followers: those who want to be with Him, and will give up their time and reputation for Him, and those who will follow Him all the way, even to the cross. He is looking for those who simply enjoy being with Him, resting in His presence. This is friendship with Jesus.

Covenantal Relationship with Jesus

Friendship with Jesus involves entering into a covenantal relationship with Him. Jesus said to His disciples before He faced the cross, that He no longer called them servants but friends. He said true friendship is when a person is willing to lay down their life for their friend (John 15:13-15). Jesus demonstrated this level of friendship when He willingly laid down His life for you and me, through His sacrifice on the cross.

During the Passover celebration at the Last Supper, Jesus invited us into a covenantal relationship with Him. After He broke the bread, He took the cup and said: *'This is My blood of the New Covenant, which is poured out for you,'* (Luke 22:20). Here, Jesus was inviting us into a blood-covenantal relationship with Him. This is the deepest form of relationship between two friends. However, since friendships are two-way, then this means we are to engage in this covenantal relationship with Him, in order for it to be valid. Just as Jesus demonstrated His sacrificial love for us on the cross, so He is inviting us to lay down our lives for Him.

Many years ago, during a time of corporate worship when we were focusing on the cross, I became overwhelmed with the presence of God. Tears were rolling down my face, and suddenly everyone around me faded in the distance as I entered in a vision.

In this vision, I saw Jesus outstretched on the cross. He seemed three times the size of a man and was looking down to me. I then heard Him speak these words to my spirit: *'Ange, I have sacrificed My life for you. Will you sacrifice your life for Me?'* Everything in my life flashed through my mind: my medical career, possessions, home, finances and relationships. Everything! Was I willing to lay it all down for Him? I saw the cost and it was huge. It was everything I had and everything that mattered to me. This was the real price I had to pay if I wanted to enter into a covenantal relationship with Jesus. I said yes to enter this covenantal relationship, where my life was no longer my own, but His.

Surrendered to Him

The Israelites didn't enter His rest, because they complained and wanted to be in charge of their own lives.

'Today if you hear His voice, **do not harden your hearts as you did in the rebellion,** *during the time of testing in the desert, where your fathers tested and tried me and for forty years saw what I did. This is why I was angry with that generation, and I said,* **'Their hearts are always going astray, and they have not know My ways.'** *So I declared an oath in My anger,* **'They shall never enter My rest''** (Hebrews 3:7-11+19).

The Israelites didn't enter God's rest because of their rebellious ways. Their complaints and selfish attitudes turned their hearts away from God. This prevented them from knowing His ways, because they didn't put their faith and trust in Him. Since they couldn't see what lay ahead, they wanted to return to their former ways of life. They feared not being in control so took back control. Fear, control, rebellion, unbelief, criticism and pride, prevented them from entering His rest.

If we want to enter His rest, then our hearts are to give the reins of fear (including anxious or doubtful thoughts), control, judgement, pride and rebellion to Him, and thus let Him reign in our hearts. Those who live a monastic life have learned how to enter His rest, by abandoning themselves daily to Him. We too can choose this lifestyle as we daily abandon our hearts to Him.

One of the reasons we may struggle to be at peace or rest, is because we strive too much by doing things in our own strength and ability, instead of yielding our hearts to God. *'You will keep in perfect peace him whose mind is steadfast, because he trusts in You'* (Isaiah 26:3). As we focus our minds on God and let Him reign in our hearts, we will experience His perfect peace.

Jesus said: ***'Come to Me** all who are weary and burdened, and **I will give you rest. Take My yoke** upon you and learn from Me, **and you will find rest for your souls**,'* (Matthew 11:28-29). This has various levels of meaning, but as we bring our issues or concerns to Him and lean on Him, then we can enter His rest. To be yoked means to be in union with Him, where we totally depend on Him, in the same way a baby is yoked to their mother.

When Moses asked God whom would He send to be with him as he led God's people into the Promised Land, He replied: *'**My Presence will go with you and I will give you rest**'* (Exodus 33:14). What a profound answer. The presence of God manifested as a cloud by day and pillar of fire by night, and led Moses through the desert. But note that the Lord added that He would give Moses 'rest'. Some believe God was referring to the Promised Land as being the place of rest. However, I believe God was referring to giving Moses spiritual rest whilst travelling along the unfamiliar paths through the desert.

This highlights the most important thing as we journey through the desert. It is not necessary that we know where we are going, but know His presence is with us. This comes as we discover His place of rest in our hearts. As the Psalmist said: *'He who **dwells in the shelter** of the Most High **will rest** in the shadow of the Almighty.'* (Psalm 91:1).

Who Will Be a Resting Place for Him?

The Lord is looking for places of habitation where He may come and dwell in our hearts. As the prophet Isaiah said: *'The **Spirit of the Lord will rest on him**'* (Isaiah 11:2). This is more than being 'filled' with the Spirit. The prophet was referring to the Lord Himself coming and making His home in us.

Jesus said: *'If anyone loves Me, he will obey My teaching. My Father will love him and* **We will come to him and make Our home with him**' (John 14:23). The Lord doesn't want to have just a trickle of our time each day or week, but rather to come and rest permanently, by making His home in us. He wants to rest in us twenty four hours a day.

This is such an honour and a privilege. What would we think or do if the Queen or King asked if they could come and stay in *our* home? My immediate thought would be, 'Why do they want to come to my 'humble,' ordinary abode? Wouldn't they want to go somewhere more grand or luxurious?' What would you do if they replied they wanted to come and stay with YOU?

Most of us would probably feel the urge to get our homes in order, and throw out the rubbish and clean the rooms. We would want the fragrance to be pleasing and welcoming. Hence, some may buy new furniture or re-decorate their rooms. The truth is King Jesus wants to come and make His resting place in me and you. He is knocking at the doors of our heart (Revelation 3:20). However, we may have to get rid of our filth, or old mindsets, or ungodly lifestyles, in order to prepare our hearts for Him. Then the King of Glory may come and enter our humble abodes. He is looking for a bride who has prepared her heart for Him (Revelation 19:7).

Heidi Baker prophesied this word in Singapore many years ago and this word is still anointed for today.

'The Lord said, "There is a lot of infection in the church that causes her not to run and I want to heal My church and close her wounds. But if I am to heal My church and close her wounds, then she needs to understand who she is. She is created as a resting place for Me. She is

created to finish well. She is created to carry My glory." Who will become a resting place for Him?' [2]

When Paul declared, *'Christ in you, the hope of all glory'* he was implying something profound (Colossians 1:27). If we look at these words, we will discover a greater depth to their meaning. The Greek word for 'in' is *'en'* [3] and implies a *relation of rest, in or upon.* Hence, it means 'Christ resting in and upon you'. Likewise, the Greek word used for 'hope,' also means expectation or confidence. And the glory refers to His manifest presence. So this could be paraphrased, 'Christ resting in and upon you, the inner confidence and expectation of His manifest presence'.

Christ wants to come and fully rest in us, so we become hosts of His manifest presence. Where will He find His resting place?

Lord, show me how to become a tabernacle for Your presence. Teach me how to enter Your Sabbath rest, so I may operate from the place of resting in Your presence. Lord, help me to become Your resting place.

ENDNOTES

[1] Shabbat (Hebrew 7676); *Strong's Expanded Exhaustive Concordance: Red Letter Edition*

[2] Heidi Baker; *The Resting Place; (sermon on youtube, Cornerstone Church Community, Singapore).*

[3] En (Greek 1722); *Strong's Expanded Exhaustive Concordance: Red Letter Edition*

Fire in the Desert

4

Overcoming Circumstances

Be joyful always; pray continually; give thanks in all circumstances, for this is God's will for you in Christ Jesus

2 Thessalonians 5:16-18

The circumstances we encounter in life can present themselves as either a blessing or a challenge. We love it when things go well, but what about when things become challenging or don't go the way we would like? How do we overcome our circumstances instead of letting our circumstances overcome us?

Paul addressed this issue when he spoke to the Thessalonians: *'Give thanks in **all** circumstances, for this is God's will for you'* (1 Thessalonians 5:18). This is because God is greater than any circumstance we face, and works for the good with those who love Him and have been called according to His purpose (Romans 8:28).

The key to overcoming our circumstances is not so much what is going on the outside, but how we respond on the inside.

Peace in the Midst of the Storm

How would we respond if we were up to our necks in the sea and huge waves were crashing over us? There are at least three choices we could make. First, we could do nothing and let the waves toss us about or drag us under the water. Second, we could position ourselves to catch the waves and surf with them to the shore. Or third, we could tackle the waves by either jumping over or diving under them.

Similarly, we could allow ourselves to be overwhelmed by our circumstances, or try to find some way through. Sometimes, we may be fighting our circumstances when it may be right to go with the flow. The storms we face may be with our work, studies, relationships, church, family, health, home or finances. How we tackle each storm will determine the outcome.

During turbulent times, we may struggle to keep our heads above the water, especially when we keep looking at the waves instead of looking to Jesus. The waves can represent ongoing issues, such as fears, anxieties, temptations, false accusations, gossip, being wrongly judged by others, sickness, and so forth.

How do we rise above these waves instead of allowing them to pull us down? God can make a way where there seems to be no way, for nothing is impossible with God. Circumstances may try to pull us down, whereas focusing our hearts and minds on God will enable us to rise above each storm.

Jesus fearlessly walked on the Sea of Galilee. When Peter saw Him walking on water, he asked if he could join Him. Jesus said, 'Come!' Peter instantly responded. This one word, 'come' was rich in meaning, for it meant; I am with you; you will not drown if you hold onto My hand and keep your eyes on Me. However, there was a condition to this promise. Peter had to step out in faith. And to do this, he had to keep his eyes focused on Jesus.

As Peter stepped out of the boat, he began to do the impossible. He walked on water. So what made him start to sink? The moment Peter took his eyes off Jesus and focused on the raging waves. Fear entered his heart and he started to sink. So he cried out to Jesus. Jesus rescued him and said: *'You of little faith, why did you doubt?'* (Matthew 14:22-31).

I was out walking one summer's evening, enjoying the serene atmosphere, when I felt an urge to soar in my spirit. I imagined myself flying through the sky on wings like eagles. As I soared in my spirit, there was such a sense of joy and freedom. This released more energy within, making me feel like wanting to fly even higher. The joy I was feeling not only lifted up my spirit, but strengthened my inner being. Instead of feeling dragged down by the things around me, I chose to rise above as my spirit soared with God's Spirit. His Spirit enables us rise above our circumstances, if we choose to live by faith and not by what we see around us (2 Corinthians 5:7). Hence, we can choose to rise above our circumstances as we look with our eyes of faith to Jesus.

There is another way to avoid being tossed about by our circumstances and this is by diving deeper into God's heart. It is as we dive deeper into His presence, that we get to experience His peace beneath the storm.

Jesus Calms the Storm

Jesus was with His disciples in a boat when a storm began to arise. Jesus was in a deep sleep, possibly resting in His Father's presence, when His disciples cried out: *'Teacher, don't You care if we drown?'* Jesus got up, rebuked the wind and commanded the waves to be quiet (Mark 4:35-40). Jesus overcame the storm by taking authority over the situation. He discerned the storm was due to spiritual opposition, and so rebuked it.

Jesus was resting in God's presence to the extent that He wasn't affected by the storm. However, He took authority over the storm for the sake of those around Him. It is the peace of God reigning in our hearts that overcomes the storms around us. We too have divine authority to rebuke the spiritual storms, when God's peace is reigning in our hearts.

Spiritual Opposition

Immediately after the storm ceased, Jesus and His disciples arrived at the region of Gadarenes where they met a demon-possessed man. The demons, named Legion, knew of Jesus' assignment, hence sent the storm to stop Him coming. Jesus discerned the storm was due to opposition, hence came against it with divine authority. Likewise, when things are hurled our way, we can ask God if it is the enemy trying to oppose us. And if so, then we can take authority by rising above it in the Spirit, because He who is in us is greater than him in the world (1 John 4:4).

The enemy is out to kill, steal and destroy what God has for us. If he can't have it, he certainly doesn't want us to. Hence, he will try to prevent us from fulfilling God's purpose and calling. The enemy begins by challenging our minds with fears, lies, doubts, uncertainties, as well as thoughts of pride and rebellion. He will even throw storms our way, like a financial crisis or serious health issues, or colleagues turning against us. He will try to make us doubt God's word and forget His promises. During times like these, we can choose to focus on the storm or rise above our circumstances by turning the eyes of our heart to God.

Overcoming Our Circumstances

Jesus never let His circumstances get the better of Him. His faith was totally in His Father. Nothing could shake Him for He didn't hold on to the things of the world. He was totally dependent on His Father for everything. He walked through life's challenges with an inner peace, because He is the Prince of peace (Isaiah 9:6). Storms or bad news didn't overwhelm Him for He always turned to His Father.

When Jesus heard about Lazarus' death, He didn't rush to the scene, but waited patiently until His Father told Him to go. He fearlessly walked through storms, commanding the waves to be quiet. All that He needed, His Father provided. When a crowd of people were about to throw Him off the cliff, He walked straight through them. As His Spirit soared above His flesh, He could effortlessly walk through such opposition. Even when He faced the cross, His Spirit overcame all that was hurled at Him. Jesus said that anyone who has faith in Him will do even greater things than Him (John 14:12). Jesus demonstrated how we can overcome our circumstances by knowing His truth, walking in faith, and trusting in His word and promises.

Overcome with the Truth

Many of us struggle with negative thoughts and lies, about God or ourselves, especially when facing difficulties. When friends betray us, we feel hurt and rejected. Or whenever we fail at something, we may think we are no good and will never make it. Or when all looks bleak and nothing seems to be happening, we think God has forgotten us. If we are not careful, this may lead us down a path of oppression or depression, as we allow negative thoughts to influence our minds. Negative thoughts may seem real but are actually based on lies and false beliefs, for they are not from God!

One way of dealing with such negative thoughts is to write them down, especially the ones we keep rehearsing in our mind (such as, 'I am a failure,' 'No-one wants to be my friend', 'Nothing will happen for me', 'They don't care about me', 'How will I get out of this mess?', 'There is no cure, I'm going to die', 'My life isn't worth living'...or perhaps negative thoughts about someone else), and then bring each negative thought or fear to God and ask Him to reveal His truth. However, we are to believe with faith that He will answer us. He has given us a Counsellor, the Holy Spirit, who is the Spirit of Truth, and we can call on Him any time of the day or night for His revelatory truth (John 15:26, 16:13).

Alternatively, we can imagine ourselves (with our eyes of faith) coming before Jesus and giving Him each negative thought and false belief. As we give Him each negative thought and fear, we can ask Him for His truth in exchange. Some may receive a word, scripture, picture, or something else. We will be pleasantly surprised when we hear His truth. Hence, we can choose to believe His truth, or partner with the fears and lies from the enemy. Whereas fears and lies will keep us in bondage, His truth will always set us free (John 8:32).

The enemy tries to pull us down with fears and lies about ourselves, God or others. God always thinks differently to us and outside the box, for His ways are not our ways and His thoughts are not our thoughts (Isaiah 55:8). God sees things differently to man. All we need to do is put on our spiritual lenses by asking God for His truth, and He will reveal things from His perspective. His words bring life, not death. Hence, we can partner with His truth instead of the lies, fears or doubts from the enemy.

There was a young woman who had developed symptoms as a result of her fears, stresses, and anxious thoughts. It had got so severe that she feared going to college. So I got her to focus her heart on Jesus and to bring all her anxieties and fears to Him. As she handed each one to Him, she let go of her emotional stress and listened to His Spirit of Truth. Tears welled up as she received His truth in exchange for each fear and lie. She had developed a self-hate because she had listened to the lies of the enemy about her looks or what others thought about her. When she gave this to Jesus she cried as she heard His truth concerning what He thought about her. She chose to accept His words, instead of the lies from the enemy. By receiving the words of truth from Jesus, she was powerfully set free.

Faith in God's Word

One of the trials Jesus faced when fasting in the desert, was the temptation to give into His hunger. Hence, satan tempted Him to turn the stones into bread. Jesus replied with the Word of God: *'It is written: "Man doesn't live on bread alone, but on every word that comes from the mouth of God,"'* (Matthew 4:4). Jesus overcame the enemy with the sword of the Spirit, the living Word of God. When we trust in His Word, He is faithful and helps us overcome whatever difficult circumstance we may face.

Abraham was considered to be a man of faith, as he held on to God's word and promises. Even when God told Abraham to offer Isaac as a sacrifice on the altar, he obeyed having faith in God's word. He believed God would make him a father of nations. He reasoned that God would somehow bring Isaac back to life, in order to fulfil this promise, and God did (Hebrews 11:17).

When God gives us a powerful word, the enemy will do everything to quench it or abort it, like bringing a storm our way. The beautiful thing is that God calls us to do the impossible and will make a way where there is no way. He doesn't operate in our logic or common-sense mindset, for His ways are not our ways (Isaiah 55:8). He made us to be spiritual beings residing in human bodies. Hence, we were created to live a naturally supernatural lifestyle. If we always do what is possible, then we will have no need for God. God wants us to take His hand, as we step out and do the outrageous things with Him.

When God told Adam and Eve, not to eat from the Tree of the Knowledge of Good and Evil, it seemed a relatively easy thing to do, until the enemy came along and persuaded Eve to eat from it. First, he challenged her mindset, putting doubt in her mind. *"Did*

God really say, 'You must not eat from any tree in the garden'?" Since doubt didn't work, the enemy tried another tactic. Next, he threw a lie attached to the temptation to be 'like God': *'You will not surely die,' the serpent said to the woman. 'For God knows that when you eat of it, your eyes will be opened and you will be like God, knowing good and evil'* (Genesis 3:2-4). The lie worked! She believed in the lie that she wouldn't die and succumbed to the temptation. She chose to listen to another voice instead of God's.

John the Baptist was sent to prepare the way for the Lord. He was a man of faith who delivered God's word, and proclaimed Christ as the Messiah. After he was arrested and thrown in prison, doubt entered his mind. He probably thought something like this: *'Is He the Christ? Then why am I in prison? How could He let this happen to me if He really is the Messiah? He eats with sinners, drinks wine and even hangs out with prostitutes. Have I got the right man?'* While these thoughts were playing on John's mind, he wisely decided to test them. He sent his disciples to Jesus to find the answer. He went to the Source Himself. Jesus' word ministered to John's spirit. On hearing the Word, He knew that Jesus was indeed the Messiah (Matthew 11:2-10).

Whenever we have a negative thought, a false belief or any doubt in God's word, we simply can go back to the Source. God will affirm His word to our spirit, and help us to walk by faith in Him.

Paul instructed Timothy to fight the good fight of the *faith*, not giving into the worldly influences around him (1 Timothy 6:12). Paul had every reason to give up his call or ministry. He faced physical and spiritual storms when he was imprisoned, beaten and stoned to death. However, others prayed and God raised him from the dead. He went for days without food or shelter and regularly faced death. Yet in all his difficulties and seemingly impossible circumstances, he held on by putting his faith in Christ, instead of putting faith in his circumstances.

'I have been in prison more frequently, been flogged more severely, and been exposed to death again and again. Five times I received from the Jews the forty lashes minus one. Three times I was beaten with rods, once I was stoned, three times I was shipwrecked, I spent a night and a day in the open sea, I have been constantly on the move. I have been in dangers from rivers, from bandits, from my own countrymen; in danger from Gentiles; in danger in the city, in danger in the country, in danger at sea; and in danger from false brothers. I have laboured and toiled and often gone without sleep; I have known hunger and thirst and often gone without food; I have been cold and naked. Beside everything else, I face daily the pressure of my concern for all the churches' (2 Corinthians 11:23-29).

During one of the storms at sea, when it seemed inevitable that everyone would die, Paul turned to God. God sent an angel and Paul said: *'Last night, an angel of the God whose I am and whom I serve, stood beside me and said, "Do not be afraid, Paul. You must stand trial before Caesar and God has graciously given you the lives of all who sail with you." So keep up your courage men,* **for I have faith in God that it will happen just as He told me'** (Acts 27:21-25).

Though Paul had been through various trials and suffered for his faith, he still gave thanks and praise to God. God is always faithful to His word. Paul overcame every impossible circumstance by putting his faith and trust firmly in God, in His spoken word and His promises.

Trust in His Promises

God will give us words of encouragement to help us through our trials or difficult circumstances. Many may receive a prophetic word concerning their destiny and future, followed by encountering tests or trials. Hence, we either allow ourselves to be overcome by trials, circumstances, or by hearing bad news, or we can overcome by declaring His promises as we focus our hearts on Him.

Fire in the Desert

'He will have no fear of bad news; his heart is steadfast, trusting in the Lord. His heart is secure, he will have no fear; in the end he will look in triumph on his foes' (Psalm 112:7-8).

Trusting in God means not leaning on our own understanding, but keeping our eyes focused on Him, regardless of what is happening around us (Proverbs 3:5-6).

There was a man who had received a prophetic word concerning God's plans for his future. Shortly after, he was diagnosed with terminal cancer. At first he doubted God's promise and blamed God for allowing this to happen. He had more faith in the doctor's word than God's promise. Then the person who gave him the word challenged him by asking who was he believing – the doctor's prognosis or God's word? He realised the Lord had given this prophetic word to help him overcome the cancer. He chose to trust in God's word and in doing so, he overcame the cancer.

When God speaks a word that is life changing, we shouldn't be surprised if trials and opposition come our way. The enemy will try every means to abort God's plans. God will have a strategy to enable us to overcome each fiery dart of the enemy. We can choose to seek Him and hold firm to His word and promises, instead of partnering with fears, lies or doubt. Sometimes, God may allow these trials to test what is in our hearts, or perhaps to strengthen our faith in Him.

Most prophetic words are conditional. That is, they will only come to pass if we do our part. For example, I may receive a prophetic word that I will be a doctor, but this means I still have to study and pass the exams. Or if I receive a word from God that I have a prophetic ministry, then I still need to train and learn how to hear and discern God's voice. Hence, if we put prophetic words from God on the shelf and do nothing, then they may not come to pass.

After we receive a specific calling from God, we usually have to go through a period of *preparation*. God has to prepare our hearts and train us through various means, so we can fulfil His purposes. David was anointed by Samuel to be the next king, but he still had to undergo thirteen years of preparation and spiritual training before he was given the crown. God tested and circumcised David's heart in every way, so he was ready to receive the crown of kingship. God is calling us to do amazing things with Him, but this may involve a season of preparation.

Holding on to Grace

As Jesus grew in stature, He also grew in wisdom and grace. *'And the child **grew and became strong**; He was **filled with wisdom** and the **grace of God was upon Him**,'* (Luke 2:40 +52). What is grace and why is it so important? Grace is God's supernatural strength and ability to do what we are unable to do in the natural. Jesus was full of grace for He lived and moved in the power of God's Spirit. He demonstrated in every test and trial that His Spirit ruled His flesh. His body and soul (mind, will and emotions) came under His Spirit, so He could overcome every trial sent His way. His strength wasn't in His flesh, but in His Spirit, as He daily surrendered to the will of His Father.

Satan asked if he could sift Peter like wheat, but Jesus prayed Peter's faith would be strong enough to overcome such trials (Luke 22:32). This sifting was a season when Peter was led through the refiner's fire, but the result would enable him to become a carrier of His glory.

Paul constantly faced trial after trial. Yet in his most trying times, he learnt something profound. He discovered that God's grace was sufficient for him.

*'**I have learned to be content whatever the circumstances.** I know what it is to be in need and what it is to have plenty. I have learned the*

secret of being content in any and every situation, whether well fed or hungry, whether living in plenty or want. **I can do everything through Him who gives me strength**' (Philippians 4:11). Paul discovered the power of grace.

God showed Paul during one of his difficult times, that His grace was sufficient for him: *'To keep me from becoming conceited because of these surpassing great revelations, there was given me a thorn in my flesh, a messenger of Satan to torment me. Three times I pleaded with the Lord to take it away from me. But He said to me:* **"My grace is sufficient for you, for my power is made perfect in weakness."** *Therefore I will boast all the more gladly about my weaknesses, so that Christ's power may rest in me,'* (2 Corinthians 12:7-9). We too can discover the power of grace, as we choose to lean on Him.

One day, the Lord gave me some insight into grace. I suddenly realised I needed His grace to do what He had called me to do. My own strength was insufficient for what lay ahead. My own abilities would not be enough because I would simply fall if I relied on them. The only way forward was to lean on Him and learn to live each moment by grace.

Shortly before Jesus faced the cross, He gave His peace to His disciples. '**Peace I leave with you; My peace I give you.** *I do not give to you as the world gives.* **Do not let your hearts be troubled and do not be afraid**' (John 14:27). The first thing Jesus said to His disciples after His resurrection was: *'Peace be with you!'* (John 20:19).

His peace enables us to walk through storms, quench fears, and rest in the knowledge that He is with us. He who is in us is greater than he who is in the world (1 John 4:4). Whose hands are we holding during the difficult times? Are we holding the enemy's hand of doubt and fear, or Jesus' hand of peace and grace?

Give Thanks in ALL Circumstances

How many of us give thanks to God in all our circumstances? I admit I struggle with this and usually moan before I consider giving thanks. Whereas moaning and complaining opens the door for the enemy, giving thanks opens the door for God to respond. Paul told the Philippians to rejoice in God always and not be anxious about anything, but present their prayers to God with *thanksgiving* (Philippians 4:4-7).

Paul faced many trials but still gave thanks and praise to God, knowing God was with him. He learnt to rest in God's peace, not his circumstances. Paul's attitude of thanks and praise raised his spirit above his circumstances. He knew God was far greater because nothing was too difficult for Him. His spirit ruled his flesh as he learnt to live for Christ and no longer himself.

Jesus gave thanks in all situations. When there wasn't enough food, He took what there was and gave thanks to His Father. *'He took the seven loaves and fish and when **He had given thanks**, He broke them and gave them to His disciples, and they in turn to the people. They all ate and were satisfied. Afterwards, the disciples picked up seven baskets of broken bread that were left over'* (Matthew 15:36).

As Jesus approached the tomb of Lazarus, He prayed and gave thanks. *'Then Jesus looked up and said, "**Father, I thank You that You have heard Me.** I knew that You always hear Me, but I said this for the sake of the people standing here, that they may believe that You sent Me"*(John 11:41). After giving thanks to His Father, He called Lazarus to come forth.

I was with a team in Africa when we were de-worming a village of children. I had around one hundred tablets (one for each child) but the children kept increasing in number. More kept coming when they heard the tablets were free. I could see we were running out and wouldn't have enough for the two hundred or more who came. So we decided to lay hands on the tablets. By faith, with thanksgiving, we continued to give them out. Every child received a de-worming tablet, down to the last tablet that was given out. The tablets must have multiplied as we kept giving them out for they simply didn't run out. The children marvelled and praised God as they too witnessed the miracle that had taken place.

I was in a meeting where we were asked to pray for a pastor who had been imprisoned for sharing his faith in a non-Christian nation. He had already served eight years in prison for speaking about Jesus in this nation. The people responded by giving God thanks and praise for this man's faith and God's calling on his life. Before the evening was over, we heard he had been released from prison!

As we give thanks to God in *all* our situations, He frees the prisoners, multiplies our food, heals the sick, and raises the dead. Giving thanks can change our circumstances. Giving thanks and praise not only opens doors for God to act but releases faith in our hearts, as we focus on God, not our circumstance.

Tell God what we Feel

Instead of allowing anger, hopelessness, disappointments, or despair, to build up in our hearts, we can go to God and tell Him what we are feeling. There have been times when I have cried out to God, vented my despair and hopelessness and asked Him, 'Where are You? Why has this happened?' So often we don't tell God how we feel. Many times I ask people if they have told God how they feel, and they reply 'no'. I encourage them to speak from their heart to Him. I believe He will reply when we truly cry out to Him, for He loves us too much not to reply to our hearts of anguish and tears.

God wants us to be authentic and real with Him. He doesn't like pretence or cover up. He knows what is in our hearts, but is waiting for us to release it all to Him. Each time I've released my emotions to Him, He has graciously ministered to my spirit and strengthened my inner being.

Hold Onto God

During my season of transition, God made it clear that I had to let go of the old ways in order to be able to take on the new. It was hard at first, because I was happy to continue with the old and didn't really want anything new. Bit by bit, as I put my faith and trust in Him, He led me step by step of the way.

Transition can be a hard time when we let go of our former ways not knowing what is next. However, we can step forward by faith and obedience, as we choose to keep our eyes on Jesus and look ahead. This is when we walk by faith as we hold on to God's hand not knowing what lies ahead.

As God led me to let go of my former ways, I entered a short period where nothing seemed to be happening. I had been waiting for God to open doors, but nothing happened. Things didn't happen the way I expected. I didn't understand why God hadn't responded. Had I heard Him right? Why had nothing opened for me? Where was God? Was He with me? Had I missed something? It was a bit like Pilgrim's Progress, where I came across 'doubt', 'confusion', 'uncertainty', 'control' and 'fear' on my journey. It made me question my call. I kept thinking that if God didn't do something then I would need to take action.

I realised I was in a battle with my flesh and spirit. God's Spirit was telling me to wait and trust in His perfect timing. He would open new doors and make fresh connections. Each time I cried out to God to respond to my situation I would sense in my spirit to just wait and rest in Him. It was a test of my faith in God as I simply lived one day at a time. He brought me into a situation where it looked impossible for anything to happen. He then spoke to my spirit and said this was a time of testing. I was to arise above my circumstances by focusing on Him. It was like when Peter stepped onto the water. If I focused on what was happening around me, I would feel despair, as if I was sinking. However, if I kept my eyes on Jesus, through prayer and worship, then I would walk through the storm. The key to getting through this season was to keep my eyes on Jesus and daily abide in His presence.

Two Trees & Two Wisdoms

One of the things that can help us through our circumstances is the wisdom of God. Wisdom is one of the gifts that God has given to help and encourage us in our circumstances (1 Corinthians 12:8). However, we mustn't forget there are two wisdoms. There is the wisdom of the world and the wisdom of God, and they are very different.

*'For the message of the cross is foolishness to those who are perishing, but to us who are being saved it is the power of God. For it is written: "**I will destroy the wisdom of the wise; the intelligence of the intelligent I will frustrate.**" Where is the wise man? Where is the scholar? Where is the philosopher of this age? Has not **God made foolish the wisdom of the world?** For since in **the wisdom of God** the world through its wisdom did not know Him....**For the foolishness of God is wiser than man's wisdom**...It is because of Him that you are in **Christ Jesus, who has become for us wisdom from God**'* (1 Corinthians 1:18-30).

There is also the Spirit of Wisdom and this is one of the seven-fold Spirits (Isaiah 11:2). Jesus is the Wisdom of God. He is the Way, the Truth, the Word and the Life. Hence, true Wisdom points us to God (Matthew 11:19, Proverbs 8:12-14). However, the wisdom of the world focuses on 'self' since it comes from the flesh. Hence, worldly wisdom comes from the mindset of man, instead of the mindset of God.

God's wisdom always directs us to Him because Wisdom is a person. It carries both revelation and truth, and brings peace and freedom. However, the wisdom of the world is based on the opinions of man, including fear and false beliefs, and this brings bondage. Likewise, the Wisdom of God is from the Tree of Life whereas the wisdom of this world is from the Tree of Knowledge of Good and Evil. King Solomon, the author of the book of Proverbs, describes wisdom in detail and that she is a tree of life to those who embrace her (Proverbs 3:18).

James said that if anyone lacks the wisdom of God then we can ask Him for it. God will give us His wisdom when we ask because He is a generous God (James 1:5). He goes on to describe God's wisdom.

'Who is wise and understanding among you? Let him show it by his good life, by deeds done in humility that comes from wisdom....the wisdom that comes from heaven is first of all pure; then peace-loving, considerate, submissive, full of mercy and good fruit, impartial and sincere' (James 3:13-18).

The wisdom of this world is deceptive, though it may appear to be real. It will stop us fulfilling our call and destiny for it is based on man's thoughts, fears, false beliefs, good ideas, insecurities, and man's ways, instead of God's ways. *'"For My thoughts are not your thoughts, neither are your ways My ways," declares the Lord. "As the heavens are higher than the earth, so are my ways higher than your ways and my thoughts higher than your thoughts"'* (Isaiah 55:8).

I asked the Lord why it was important to be wise and faithful in these End-Times, as we read in the parables of the faithful servants and wise virgins (Matthew chapt 24 and 25), and this is what I wrote:

'The wise are those who seek My ways, who live in My truth. They seek My Kingdom instead of the kingdoms on earth, and know the world is

folly and futile, because man's thoughts are not My thoughts. The wise are those who pursue righteousness, Godliness (holiness) and seek understanding and revelation from My Spirit.

The faithful are those who obey My will until the very end. They carry out My commands and fear My Name. They do only as I say or ask, and follow My Spirit. They trust in My Name and My promises, and know I am with them. I am their Helper, Provider, Shield and Friend. They know they belong to Me, they are My bond-servant, My sons and daughters, and My bride. They will say 'yes' whatever the cost, obeying My will until the very end. This is because their lives are no longer their own, but Mine, because they know they belong to Me.'

Whatever we are facing in life, whatever storm we are going through, or desert we are crossing, God will lead us through if we keep our eyes focused on Him and listen to His Spirit. He will give us His wisdom and understanding, whenever we ask. His perfect peace overcomes all our fears, when our minds are stayed on Him.

Lord Jesus, forgive me when I have taken my eyes off You and focused too much on my circumstances. Forgive me when I have doubted Your word and promises. Help me to keep my eyes on You and seek Your wisdom, instead of the wisdom of the world.

5

Refiner's Fire

*I counsel you to buy from Me gold
refined in the fire so you can become rich*

Revelation 3:18

The desert is a place where we encounter the school of 'self-discovery'. This is known amongst the monastic people as the school of 'self-awareness'. During these seasons we discover more about God's nature and character, and also about our *self*.

Most of us are not aware of our character flaws until others or the Lord may draw them to our attention. Becoming aware is simply the first step. Developing the right attitude of heart is the next. As we surrender the various facets of our 'self' to Him, we will become less 'self-focused' and more 'self-aware'.

Self-awareness is when we become more aware of our own reactions and behaviours, and learn to become more sensitive to those around us. In other words, God reveals what's in our hearts to help us change, so we may love and see others the way He does.

Sometimes, God may bring certain people across our path to show us how to see them through His eyes instead of our flesh. After the Lord teaches us something, He may test our hearts to see if we have developed the right attitude or response. Until we develop the right response in our hearts, He will take us around the mountain again. Many of us may not respond the first, second, or third time, but God graciously brings the same tests our way until our hearts make the right response. This is the process where He lovingly refines our hearts.

Some years ago, I used to think negatively or judgmentally towards certain people, until one day the Lord convicted my heart. I repented of my judgmental attitude and asked the Lord to help me see each one through his eyes. It was amazing what followed, for the Lord revealed to my heart how He saw them. This changed my attitude and approach towards them, when I saw them through the eyes and heart of God.

The Lord wants us to see people through His eyes and heart, because it will transform the way we respond or behave towards others.

Turn our Hearts to God

The Hebrew word for desert or wilderness is *midbar*[1]. Interestingly, this word can also mean 'speech.' Hence, the desert is a place where God speaks to our hearts. Though we may feel alone and isolated, God is as close to us in the desert as He is on the mountain top. It is just we don't *feel* His presence as much in the desert. This is because the desert is a time for us to walk by faith and not by sight (2 Corinthians 5:7).

It is more tempting to default to the ways of the world and follow what others may say, especially when God seems distant. However, this is the broad path that leads to deception and destruction. Instead, we can choose the narrow path, the one least travelled that goes against the flesh and ways of man. It is the path of Life that leads us closer to God.

Jesus said: *'Enter through the narrow gate. For wide is the gate and broad is the road that leads to destruction, and many enter through it. But small is the gate and narrow the road that leads to life, and only a few find it,'* (Matthew 7:13).

One day, when I was studying for my medical exams, I felt a tap on my shoulder. I looked but there was no-one in the room. Then I felt it again. I somehow knew God was getting my attention. So, I put down my pen and decided to go for a walk. As I started to walk, I immediately felt His presence surround me, as if He was walking with me. The sun was shining on the broad path and many were walking along it. However, after I walked past a dark, narrow and dingy looking path, I no longer felt His presence. So I back tracked my steps and decided to go down this narrow uninviting path. As soon as I did, His presence returned. He said to my spirit, He was calling me down the narrow path, a road few would take, but I had nothing to fear, for He was with me. All I needed to do was to listen to Him and be guided by His Spirit. I would know if it was the right path, for His presence would be with me. The safest place we can ever be is in the centre of God's will and His presence.

Many times, I have struggled to know where to go next or what path to take. Each time I have turned to God to show me His way. Sometimes, I have had to wait for His next steps. The narrow path follows the wisdom of God, whereas the broad path follows the wisdom of the world. God's ways are not our ways and His thoughts are not our thoughts. Worldly wisdom appears 'good', though it is foolish compared to God's wisdom. This is because it is rooted in fear, control, deception, and is often self-focused.

A fact may not necessarily be the truth. This is especially the case if a fact happens to be based on man's opinion or worldly wisdom.

However, the wisdom of God is based on revelatory truth, because it comes from God's Spirit (1 Corinthians 1:25-29). Hence, we are to be seekers of His divine truth, instead of relying on the wisdom of this world or facts based on man's opinion.

During the Corona virus outbreak, there was a pandemic of fear as a result of what was conveyed through the main news and social media. I believe that many of the so called 'facts' were based on misrepresentation and misinterpretation of data. However, all we needed to do was to turn our eyes and ears to God and ask for His truth concerning the outbreak. What was really going on, and what was our response to be? Jesus is the Truth and will gladly reveal His Spirit of truth to those who ask (John 14:6). His truth sets us free from fear, since fear is *false evidence appearing real.*

We are not meant to be slaves to fear, but to turn our hearts to our Father, as we seek His Spirit and truth. *'You did not receive a spirit that makes you a slave again to fear, but you received the Spirit of sonship'* (Romans 8:15).

Refiner's Fire

As you know, plants tend to yield more flowers and fruit if they are regularly pruned. I've noticed that if I don't prune my plants some may go on to develop diseases, like 'powdery mildew', 'black spot' or 'rust', and this may then spread to the surrounding plants. Such plants require pruning to remove the disease and also prevent further spread.

Likewise, the Lord may take us through pruning seasons so we may yield more fruit for Him in His Kingdom (John 15:2). However, a pruning season may feel like going through a refiner's fire. As He leads us through His fire, He will gently break and melt the hardened or ungodly areas in our hearts. These may be areas such as, pride, selfishness, fear of man, control, false beliefs, false securities, unforgiveness, or whatever requires pruning.

Though the times of pruning may feel uncomfortable, He gives us the grace to walk through such seasons. For some, it may feel like the heat has been turned up to a higher temperature. For others, it may feel like being sieved or tested to higher standards (Luke 22:31). However, unless we allow the Lord to deal with our carnal nature, then it may simply get in the way and lead to our downfall.

On some occasions, God has led me through His refiner's fire. On one occasion, I had just finished a season of medical outreaches in Mozambique, when I felt His Spirit prompt me to take a two week fast. His grace enabled me to fast during this time. In the Spirit, I saw Jesus was taking my hand and leading me through what looked like a refiner's fire. The flames appeared tall, like walls of fire. Every other day, I found myself breaking-down in tears, as God touched different areas in my heart. During these two weeks, the Lord was refining my heart from prideful thoughts. At the end of the two weeks I knew it was finished. He had been preparing my heart for the next assignment, and this required a humble, obedient heart.

After Job encountered the refiner's fire, he finally came out bearing new shoots. *'At least there is hope for a tree: If it is cut down, it will sprout again, and its new shoots will not fail. Its roots may grow old in the ground and its stump die in the soil, yet at the scent of water it will bud and put forth shoots like a plant,'* (Job 14:7-9).

Being sifted is an extreme form of refining, for nothing is allowed to remain that is not of Him. It is a bit like the distilling of wine. In order for the wine to mature to a high standard, it has to be sieved until there are no more dregs or sediment left. The reason the Lord may take us down this path is simply for our hearts to be prepared for His greater purposes and callings.

The Lord lovingly rebukes and disciplines us, because He wants us to share in His holiness (Hebrews 12:7-11). He is knocking on the door of our hearts, so we may invite Him in and He may fellowship with us (Revelation 3:20).

Here are some of the areas He may lovingly refine in our hearts, to enable us to draw closer to Him.

Dependency & Security

There was a time when the Lord lovingly took away the things that mattered in my life, and then asked me this question: *'Ange, am I enough?'* It was then I realised that I had been relying on others to meet my needs instead of God. God wanted me to hold onto Him, not with one but with both of my hands. This meant I had to let go of the other things I was holding onto, in order to fully hold onto Him.

Many of us may think we depend on God, but the test comes when He begins to take away our securities. He will show us our 'crutches' and remove them one by one until we become fully yielded to Him. Our crutch may be a sickness (or diagnosis), a spouse, a job, finances, or something or someone we have chosen to lean on more than we lean on Him. Hence, our crutches may provide a false sense of comfort, identity and security.

When God begins to take away the things we have been relying on more than Him, He is simply removing our false crutches. Instead, He is teaching us how to lean on Him as we begin to trust Him to meet our needs.

Lord, reveal the false crutches or false securities in my life that You want to address. Give me grace to surrender these to You and put my trust in You.

Identity

When we are in the desert we may be faced with the thought, 'Who am I?' Jesus was challenged twice by Satan about His identity whilst in the desert (Matthew 4: 3+6).

The reason we may be challenged about our identity may be because we have taken on a false identity, based on what we do or who we know. A woman commented after her husband died that she didn't know who she was anymore or where she belonged. Others may struggle with their identity when they no longer work or become unemployed.

One day, the Lord asked me to take off my medical hat and give it to Him, because He didn't see me as a doctor, but as His daughter. What matters is how He sees us and for us to discover our true identity in our relationship with Him. The Lord wants us to discover how He sees us, so we don't seek our identity in our work or who we know, but in Him alone.

Lord, remove any false identity I have come under and reveal my true identity in You. Lord, show me how You see me.

Pride

For many, the desert may be the place where God exposes our pride as He takes us through a season of brokenness. The Lord may break the pride or ego in our hearts that is preventing us from going deeper with Him. Just as pride made satan fall, so it will make us fall. Pride covers a multitude of sins such as, self-reliance, self-righteousness, self-ambition, self-focus, selfishness, self-pity, self-defence, self-opinion, vanity, self-gain, self-reward, self-promotion, my rights, and so forth.

The Lord revealed areas where there was pride in my heart and how this was blocking my relationship with Him and with others. I was not aware of this until He revealed certain things where pride was the root. He took me through a season of brokenness, as I repented for each prideful thought and asked Him to change my heart. There were many tears as His Spirit lovingly tenderised my heart.

Lord, deal with any areas of pride or rebellion in my heart. Give me a tender, loving heart, so my heart may beat in rhythm with Your heartbeat.

Release Control

Some of us may feel the need to *always* be in control and struggle when we don't have the control reins. This isn't a healthy form of control, and in such cases the Lord may ask us to release the control reins to Him. This is not to be confused with 'self-control' which is a fruit of the Spirit (Galatians 5:23). Self-control is where we control our 'self'. That means we have control over our tongue, body and actions. This is different to always wanting to be in control or to control others.

Control is linked to fear, for we may start to fear or panic when we no longer feel in control. Many of us have been challenged by the Lord to stop striving or doing things in our own strength, and release our control reins to Him. This is another area to be refined in our hearts, as we learn to trust Him, by fully surrendering our control reins to Him.

One of the areas in my heart that I struggled with whilst in the desert was the fear of not knowing what lay ahead and having no control on what was happening. During this struggle, the Lord asked me to release the control reins to Him and let go of my fear of the future. Did I trust Him enough to do this? Could I trust Him with my life and was I willing to surrender my life to Him? The Lord was refining this area in my heart because He wanted me to fully put my whole trust and confidence in Him. This is part of growing in sonship, when we no longer choose to hold on to fear, but to hold His hand as we walk with Him (Romans 8:15).

Lord Jesus, reveal the areas of ungodly control in my heart and help me to surrender these to You. Teach me how to respond in each situation, so I am no longer a slave to fear, but respond from a relationship of sonship with You.

Guard our Hearts & Mouths

Many of us may speak negative or careless words without realising the power they may have on others or ourselves. Negative words can be like curses. Hence, we are to be aware of what comes out of our mouths and guard what we carry in our hearts, for out of the overflow of the heart the mouth speaks.

God wants us to speak from His heart instead of from a critical, judgmental, angry, or wounded heart. The words we speak from our mouth are important to God. James stresses how we can praise God one moment and then curse the next (James 3:9).

It is easy to be critical and judgmental if we have an orphan heart, especially when we feel hurt, cheated, rejected or wounded. The Lord showed me that the words I speak are like a sword coming out from my mouth, because they carry power and authority. Therefore, I have to be careful of what I say, and quick to repent of any negative words or 'curses' I may speak. It is a spiritual discipline to be quick to listen, slow to speak and slow to become angry (James 1:19).

Peter said: *'Be self-controlled and alert. Your enemy the devil is prowling around like a roaring lion looking for someone to devour'* (1 Peter 5:8). Hence, we are to guard our hearts and minds, so we do not come into agreement with the enemy's language and schemes.

One way to overcome negative speech is to go on a 'negative speech fast' for a month or more. For every negative word spoken, a coin can be put in a jar. Also, it can help by asking friends or family members to point out any negative words we may speak. It can be a form of spiritual exercise to help rewire our minds and prevent us speaking negative words about others or ourselves.

Lord, convict me of any negative words that may come out of my mouth. Cleanse my mind and heart so my words may be pleasing to You.

Flesh versus Spirit

I was in a refining season when the Lord revealed how much my flesh was warring with my spirit. My flesh wanted to do one thing and my spirit wanted to do the opposite. Our flesh is at war with the spirit until we yield our flesh to God. Jesus gave little attention to His flesh because He lived a Spirit-led life. His Spirit ruled His flesh. Likewise, He taught us not to strive or operate from our flesh, but do everything through His Spirit reigning in us. He said the flesh counts for nothing but the Spirit gives life (John 6:63).

Most of us struggle with the flesh because we want to do things in our own strength or 'my way'. There is the human need to 'do' or to 'achieve' so we may feel good at the end of a day. This can be overcome when we yield to the power of His Spirit instead of our flesh.

Paul beautifully put it together in this passage: *'Those who are motivated by the flesh only pursue what benefits themselves. But those who live by the impulses of the Holy Spirit are motivated to pursue spiritual realities. For the mind-set of the flesh is death, but the mind-set controlled by the Spirit finds life and peace. In fact, the mind focused on the flesh fights God's plans and refuses to submit to His direction, because it cannot! For no matter how hard they try, God finds no pleasure with those who are controlled by the flesh. But when the Spirit of Christ empowers your life, you are not dominated by the flesh but by the Spirit,'* (TPT Romans 8:5-7).

The Lord is inviting us to invest our lives in Him and not the things of the world. Instead of seeking after riches or the things of the flesh, He is inviting us to lay it all down for Him.

Lord, help me to overcome my flesh and live a Spirit-led life. Reveal the ongoing battles in my flesh, so I may surrender these areas to You.

Obey God amidst Opposition

One of the things that made Saul fall was when he feared man more than he feared God. Many people pleasers don't like saying 'no' to others, or having to confront someone. When we are more concerned about the response from others than the response from God, we are putting the fear of man before the fear of God. In other words, we fear being rejected by man more than being rejected by God.

Peter struggled with the fear of man, especially when he denied Jesus three times. He feared being arrested, losing his reputation and even his life. He became broken-in-heart after he realised what he had done. Something happened to his spirit when Jesus ministered to his heart and reinstated his call (John 21:15-19). From then on, he chose to obey God, whatever the cost (Acts 4:19, 5:29).

David sought his strength in the Lord when his own men opposed him. Instead of giving into fear, he turned to God and obeyed His will. As a result of his obedience, he overcame opposition and turned the hearts of his men back to him.

Lord Jesus, forgive me for wanting to please man more than You. Remove any fear of man and help me to obey Your will, whatever the cost.

Crucify Our Flesh

The desert is the perfect place where God can crucify our flesh. Since our flesh eats away at our spirit, God may lovingly lead us in the desert to expose these areas of our carnal nature. Our flesh is our worst enemy, for it is at war with our spirit. When we think in the flesh, speak in the flesh, act in the flesh or listen with the flesh, then we will say or do things that are contrary to God. Not only that, but our flesh will quench our spirit and this may cause us to fall. The only way we can overcome our flesh is by daily surrendering our hearts to Christ.

If we truly want to follow Him and surrender our lives to Him, then at some point in our journey with Him we will encounter the cross. The cross is the place of total surrender to His Spirit, as we yield the areas of 'self' to Him. We don't have to go looking for this because the Lord Himself will invite us to lay down our lives for Him.

The late Jill Austin[2] wrote this prophetic word about the price behind the anointing: *'I'm calling you to come into the high fires to let My glory fall upon you, but it will cost you,' He says. 'You will have to die to your reputation, your theology, and all your 'religious formulas'. You will have to let go of your fears and your control. Do you love Me enough to come?'*

She continues by describing the Master Potter creating various vessels with His hand and placing them in the kiln. *'Once again the fire moves through the kiln- but this time it's more intense. As the fire becomes a brilliant consuming yellow, you move quickly from a time of testing into a time of death. There are impurities in each vessel that only fire can cleanse. One of those impurities is competition. 'You've been comparing yourselves to each other' says the Lord. 'I will purge out that need for position.' And as the fire gets hotter He says, 'I'm purging out your religious intellect and your critical nature...' Then at the exact second you're sure you are going to die, the Lord opens all the dampers. You are no longer looking through the haze of ego, pride or religiousness. As the resurrection light of the Lord fills the kiln, you can see with new clarity in the Spirit.'*[3]

Paul experienced something similar when he spoke these words: *'I have been crucified with Christ and I no longer live, but Christ lives in me'* (Galatians 2:20). Paul had been on a journey with Jesus, where his flesh had been crucified. Hence, after he died to his complete self, he experienced the awesome presence of God living in him.

After God deals with one area, we may think it is finished, until He takes us through another area and another. After God had been operating on certain parts of my heart, I was keen to return to the mission field. However, God was still refining my heart. There was more to come. This felt the hardest season I had been through, harder than life on the mission field itself! It was as if God was working through different layers and areas I was not aware existed. At one point, I became desperate inside feeling dejected when God kept silent. It felt like He had abandoned me. I cried out, 'God, where are You? Why have You abandoned me?'

It felt like I was experiencing a complete death to self. I was willing to go through this, if it meant entering a fully resurrected life in Him. When I asked the Lord what He was doing, He spoke these words:

'My Love, it feels like doom and gloom right now, but I am letting you go through a complete death to self, so My resurrection glory may abide in you. This is the price- seek no fame, no reputation, no 'ministry' for it is all about walking with Me and abiding in Me!! Your life is with Me- do you trust Me with it? I created you and have your future mapped out! Walk by faith, obedience, abiding in My love and presence, and no longer be pulled by this world.'

After experiencing what felt like the crucifying of self, I entered a season experiencing the fullness of His joy. I began laughing in the Spirit and simply enjoyed His presence whenever I prayed.

Jesus endured the cross for the joy that was set before Him (Hebrews 12:2). Before His death, He prayed for His disciples to receive the *full measure* of joy (John 15:11, John 17:13).

From Seed to Fruit

Before a plant can bear fruit, first a seed has to fall in the ground. Each seed requires regular sunlight and water in order to grow into a seedling and then a young shoot. It then keeps growing until it is of sufficient height or maturity to produce flowers. And as we know, most flowers produce fruit. Each fruit has a seed or multiple seeds to reproduce and eventually to go on and produce a harvest.

Likewise, a seed from the fruit of the Spirit has to be sown in our hearts. After this, it goes on to be nurtured by the Word and Spirit of God, so it may continue to grow and mature until it produces fruit. The fruit can then be given away and sown in the hearts of others.

Jesus spoke these words before His death: *'Unless a kernel of wheat falls to the ground and dies, it remains only a single seed. But if it dies, it produces many seeds. The man who loves his life will lose it, while the man who hates his life in this world will keep it for eternal life. Whoever serves Me must follow Me; and where I am My servant will also be. My Father will honour the one who serves Me,'* (John 12:24-28).

When Jesus spoke these words He was referring to His death on the cross, but He was also calling us to follow Him by laying down our lives for Him. Hence, we will remain a single seed unless we are willing to yield our lives to Him.

The fruit of the Spirit begins in seed formation in our hearts, as we yield different areas of our 'self' to God. The fruit may be grace, humility, love, generosity, joy, peace, gentleness, patience and self-control (Galatians 5:22, Colossians 3:12-15). Hence, spiritual growth and maturity can be witnessed by the fruit that is produced in our hearts.

One day, as I was waiting on the Lord, I had a picture of white flour that had been ground from grains of wheat. It was the finest of flour, because it had been refined and purified. Then the Lord spoke these words that I believe are for us all:

'You have been refined and purified, broken and crushed, and now become white, pure flour that is ready to be given to others. Flour makes bread, and with the yeast of My Spirit and anointing, it will arise. I am raising you up. You are not to be 'self-raising' flour, but wait for Me to raise you up. I will expand and raise up My beautiful bride, and you (plural) will strengthen and grow beyond limits. You will overflow as you carry My presence and anointing.

*What you offer to others is My bread, My living word, which will bring life, healing and freedom. I am the bread of Life. He who eats My flesh and drinks My blood will have everlasting life. The hungry will be fed by Me. My manna will revive, sustain and bring healing and freedom. My word is Truth - it sets the captives free. So, wait, and I will pick up the flour to make bread to feed My people. As you remain broken and poured out for Me, as a daily offering of yourself, I will use you to feed and heal My people. So **do not become 'self-raising' flour** but **abide in Me** and **let My Spirit (yeast) raise you up to feed My people.**'*

When we allow Him to crucify the various areas of our flesh, then our spirit may enter a fully resurrected life in Him.

Lord Jesus, refine my heart, so I may grow deeper in my relationship with You. Tenderise my heart and crucify my flesh, so it is no longer I who lives, but You who lives in me.

END NOTES

[1] Midbar (4057 Hebrew); Strong's Exhaustive Concordance: Red Letter Edition

[2] Jill Austin; *www.lastdaysministries.org*

[3] Jill Austin; In the Hands of the Master Potter; The Price Behind the Anointing; *www.lastdaysministries.org* (2007)

6

Highway of Holiness

A Highway will be there; it will be called the Way of Holiness.

Isaiah 35:8

One of the reasons God takes us through the desert is to do a deeper work of sanctification in our hearts. When God spoke to Moses on Mount Sinai, He was calling His people to be a *kingdom of priests* and *a holy nation* (Exodus 19:6). These same words are sung by the elders and four living creatures in the Book of Revelation:

*'You are worthy to take the scroll and to open its seals because You were slain and with Your blood You purchased men for God from every tribe and language and people and nation. You have made them to **be a kingdom and priests to serve our God**, and they will **reign on the earth**'* (Revelations 5:10).

The priesthood isn't just for some but I believe it is for all. We are all called to be priests. It is not necessarily referring to the leadership of a church, but rather referring to a lifestyle of holiness. Peter confirmed this when he said: *'But you are a chosen* *people, **a royal priesthood, a holy nation,** a people belonging to God,'* (1 Peter 2:9).

Our heavenly Father has adopted us in His royal family to become royal sons and daughters in His Kingdom. Therefore, since our heavenly Father is holy, that means we are to be holy. *'But just as He who called you is holy, so be holy in all you do; for it is written: "Be holy, for I am holy,"'* (1 Peter 1:15-16).

God disciplines us out of His love, so that we may share in His holiness: *'For what son isn't disciplined by his father? If you are not disciplined (and everyone undergoes discipline), then you are illegitimate children and not true sons. Moreover, we have all had human fathers who have disciplined us and we have respected them for it. How much more then should we submit to the Father of our spirits and live! Our fathers disciplined us for a little while, as they thought best; but **God disciplines us for our good, that we may share in His holiness**,'* (Hebrews 12:8-10).

One day, I was out walking along the coast of Mozambique, and noticed how the landscape dramatically changed as I kept walking. The landscape started off as a typical sandy beach but after I climbed over an area of rocks, it changed into something that looked like an oasis. As the sun shone on the sea, it appeared beautiful and majestic, and I felt I was feasting on the wine of the Spirit. However, as I continued to walk, the landscape changed again, and appeared very different.

Suddenly, I approached a large area of rocky, desert-like ground. Since the tide was out, I could walk across this vast area of dry ground. It felt as if I was walking across a desert. Though there was no visible path, I managed to walk straight across as I fixed my eyes on the other side. However, I realised how easy it can be to go around in circles and never make it across, unless we keep our eyes on Jesus and follow the promptings of His Spirit.

After I walked across this rocky area resembling a desert, I soon put my feet onto golden sands again. However, these sands looked vastly different to the sands where I started. The stretch of beach was glistening as the sun shone on the shallow crevices of water that lay in the sand.

As I continued walking, I noticed a significant landmark on the shore that you couldn't see unless you had walked right up to this point. Right at this point, as I turned, looking out towards the sea, the sun was shining magnificently on the ocean, and the bright rays created a path of radiant light that continued along the beach, shining directly in front of me. The light was reflecting off the crevices of water along the ripples in the sand. As I turned towards this path of magnificent light, the following words came straight to my mind: 'This is the Way, walk in it!'

This coastal walk was like journeying along the path of Life. What started as an ordinary path soon became a Spirit-filled oasis, where I encountered God's presence. This then led to a barren desert where there was no visible path for me to follow. Many could get lost in this desert by walking around in circles, unless they allowed the Spirit to lead them the way through. Finally, the last part was like stepping into the anointing or glory-presence of God. Those who made it this far were living a life of radical faith and obedience to His Spirit. They had abandoned their lives to Him through encountering His cross, and were now living a resurrected life as they moved in the realms of His glory.

Sanctified Hearts

We are all on a journey of salvation. Being saved or born-again is simply the beginning of our salvation. Hence, Paul said we are to continue to work out our salvation with fear and trembling (Philippians 2:13). Our salvation is a journey of sanctification, as we draw closer to the heart of God.

Robes of Righteousness

Joshua, the high priest, was accused by satan for his unrighteous ways. He was wearing filthy clothes that were stained with sin. The Lord not only forgave his sins, but exchanged his filthy clothes with rich garments. His rich garments probably included the robe of righteousness. However, this meant Joshua was to walk in God's ways and obey His commands (Zechariah 3:1-7).

God longs to give His children new garments to wear, including the robe of righteousness, but first we have to take off our filthy garments and give them to Him. No-one would put on clean clothes without having first removed their dirty clothes. Clean garments are put on clean bodies. Likewise, the Lord cleanses us of sin and defilement, through the power of His blood, so we may put on His garments of righteousness and holiness. Those who walk in righteousness are the ones who do what is right in the eyes of the Lord. This is a lifestyle of holiness as we choose to walk in His ways and follow His commands.

It is the righteous who live by faith (Galatians 3:11, Habakkuk 2:4), and righteousness leads to holiness (Romans 6:16-19). Hence, righteousness is about doing what is right in the eyes of God as we walk along His path. As David said: *'He guides me in paths of righteousness for His name's sake'* (Psalm 23:3). His Spirit will lead us along the right path, as we choose to walk in His ways.

The more we draw closer to God, the more we become aware of His awesome holy presence. His love not only convicts our hearts but sanctifies our inner being, as we choose to follow Him.

Idolatry

Some of us may idolise things in our hearts, especially if we put 'things', 'people' or 'ministries' before God. Idolatry is when we worship something, or allow something to come before our relationship with God. This may apply to the 'love' of money, possessions, people, work, organisations, or ministries, especially when we allow them to take priority in our lives. God gives us money, food, possessions, relationships, power and ministry, but not at the expense of our relationship with Him. Without realising, we may allow things to take priority, instead of making God our priority (Revelation 2:4).

The Lord is calling His bride to make Him the centre of her life, so He may dwell in her. He is calling us to become hosts of His presence, as we choose to dwell in Him.

'Behold, I am standing at the door, knocking. If your heart is open to hear My voice and you open the door within, I will come into you and feast with you, and you will feast with Me' (Revelation 3:20 TPT).

One way to find out if there is anything we 'idolise' is to ask this question: what *can't* I give up or live without in my life? If there is anything that comes to mind, then this can be surrendered to God and see what He does or says in return. The Lord usually asks us to lay down the things we idolise that have come in the way of our relationship with Him. Some things He will give us back and other things He will take away. He does this because of His love for us.

Unforgiveness

All of us, in some way or other, have at some point experienced hurts and pains. We may have been betrayed, rejected, laughed at, lied about, let down, misunderstood, beaten, neglected, ill treated, bad words spoken about us, and the list goes on. Along with the hurt and pain, come resentment, hate, self-hate, bitterness, anger, jealousy and judgement. These become like dirty stains until we repent of our negative attitudes and forgive ourselves or those who have mistreated or hurt us. This stain of unforgiveness can go deep and spread throughout our bodies like a toxin. It may even manifest as a physical pain in the body.

The author of the book of Hebrews addressed such matters: '*Make every effort to **live in peace** with all men and **to be holy; without holiness no one will see God***. See to it that no-one misses the grace of God and that **no bitter root grows up to cause trouble and defile many**,' (Hebrews 12:14-16).

When we choose to forgive from our hearts, God can cleanse us from any bitter-root-judgement that has spiritually defiled us, and in exchange He gives us His peace. Unforgiveness is like dirt on our lenses, where we see people through the lenses of hate, anger, resentment and judgement, instead of through the lenses of God's love.

Hence, we can ask God to purify our hearts if we want to see Him. Jesus said: '*Blessed are the pure in heart for they will see God*,' (Matthew 5:8). Forgiveness becomes possible when we ask God to cleanse our lenses so we may see others or ourselves through His eyes, as we forgive from our hearts.

False Security

False security may be a form of idolatry when we rely more on people or things instead of God. For example, we may look to people to meet our needs or be our security, instead of turning our hearts to God. Or perhaps we depend on sources of income or financial assets and wealth for security and support. Sometimes the church can be our false support or security, when we rely more on others instead of God. God wants us to help and support one another in love, but that is different to looking to others for our security and support, instead of looking to Him.

I had a vivid dream where I was in a house with my parents, and saw my mother wearing a long dark cloak that covered her entire body. I noticed she also had a stutter. So I offered to pray for her stutter to be healed. Next, my father came on the scene as I was praying for my mother's stutter. He discerned she was hiding something under her dark cloak, so he tore off her cloak. Underneath the cloak was a plastic mannequin leg. This had been her crutch or false support that she was hiding from others. She was embarrassed and ashamed when this was exposed. The dream then ended.

So I asked the Lord the meaning of this vivid dream. He revealed my mother represented the body of Christ and my father represented Father God. The body of Christ was hiding behind 'false images' and 'false crutches' for their support, instead of coming to Father God for their support. The stutter was the struggle to communicate or deliver the word of God with accuracy, because the body of Christ was not depending on Him as their Source.

I believe God wants us to totally depend on Him and lean on Him for our support, as we put our confidence in His Spirit. He no longer wants us to talk *about* Him, but to deliver His word smoothly, so it flows straight from His Spirit through our mouths to the hearts of His people.

Enemy Strongholds

There are different *enemy strongholds* that we may struggle with (for example pride, fear, unbelief, control, rebellion, greed, selfishness, sexual issues, judgement, insignificance, passivity, criticism, and so on). We can invite the Holy Spirit to expose our strongholds and show us His ways to overcome.

In a vision, the Lord showed me a path. This path represented the Highway of Holiness, and along it ran the river of Life. On each side of this path were hills that represented empires. However, I saw the empires were not attached to the river of Life. Then I noticed there were flat areas around this path. These flat areas formed a network as they reached out to the surrounding communities, but I saw they were connected to the river of Life.

The Lord showed me how there are many empires built by man that are called churches, but they are not connected to His river of Life. They are focused on doing their own thing and building their own empire, instead of building God's Kingdom (Haggai 1:2-13). Hence, instead of reaching outwards, they grow taller.

However, the flat areas were also churches, and smaller fellowship groups. They were flat because they didn't focus on building 'self' but chose to focus on the people in their surrounding communities. These were linked to the river of Life, for His Spirit was flowing through them and touching the people. These increased by spreading outwards as they further advanced the Kingdom.

Fear of the Lord

Holiness goes hand in hand with the fear of the Lord. They are like brother and sister, or opposite sides of a coin. Hence, where there is a lack of the fear of the Lord, there is usually a lack of holiness. To understand God's holiness requires the fear of the Lord. If we lack it, then we can ask Him for it.

To fear the Lord is to revere Him. Whenever I sense His awesome, holy presence, I just want to kneel or bow down before Him. It's as if the King of kings has entered the room and there is a silence, as we encounter His awesome, holy presence.

When God appeared to Moses in the form of a burning bush, He said: *'Take off your sandals, for the place where you are standing is holy ground,'* (Exodus 3:5). Whenever I come into God's awesome presence, I choose to honour Him by taking off my shoes, since I am standing in His holy presence.

Holiness is an attitude of our heart when we stand in God's presence. *'And a highway will be there; it will be called the Way of*

Holiness. The unclean will not journey on it; it will be for those who walk in that Way,' (Isaiah 35:8).

Lord Jesus, sanctify my mind, will, and emotions, through the cleansing power of Your blood. Wash away the dirt or stains from my eyes and heart, so I may see others as You want me to. Teach me Your ways and how to fear Your name, so I may walk along the Way of Holiness with You.

Fire in the Desert

7

Spiritual Breakthrough

*One who breaks open the way will go up before them;
they will break through the gate and go out*

Micah 2:13

There may be times when we feel we are in a spiritual desert and are desperate for a breakthrough. It may be a breakthrough in our health, work, family, relationships, finances, church, ministry, or our personal walk with God. Here are some tools to help us break through.

Praying with Others

There have been some times when I have felt like throwing in the towel and giving up the fight, but the thing that has helped me persevere has been fellow prayer warriors standing beside me. Their prayers have helped to strengthen my faith and fight off any weariness, doubt, disappointment or unbelief. One man can put a thousand to flight but two men can put ten thousand to flight (Deuteronomy 32:30). God encourages us to stand with one another in prayer, so battles may be won. Jesus said when two or more gather together in His name, He is with us (Matthew 18:20).

Joshua overcame the Amalekites because Moses stood praying for him. As Moses interceded for Joshua, he too needed support. Hence, Aaron and Hur were there to uphold Moses arms:

'So Joshua fought the Amalekites as Moses had ordered, and Moses, Aaron and Hur went to the top of the hill. As long as Moses held up his hands, the Israelites were winning, but whenever he lowered his hands, the Amalekites were winning. When Moses hands grew tired, they took a stone and put it under him and he sat on it. Aaron and Hur held his hands up- one on one side, one on the other- so that his hands remained steady until sunset' (Exodus 17:8).

Breakthrough occurred as a result of Moses standing and interceding for Joshua's battle. It was interesting how Moses was in a position to see what was happening from standing on the 'prayer hill', and he prayed until the battle was won, or breakthrough had occurred. However, just like Moses needed support, so we may need others to cover us in prayer, as we minister or pray for others.

One day, as I was having a coffee with two friends in a cafe, we noticed a woman sitting opposite who wore a wizard's hat. It seemed she wanted our attention so we started to chat to her. It turned out she was a witch and practiced all sorts of 'healing' by conjuring spells. So we testified to there being a greater Source of energy to heal the sick and His name was the Holy Spirit. She then realised we were Christians. She commented that since there were three of us, she wasn't going to test her source of power with ours, because she knew that three were more powerful than one. We smiled as we silently interceded for her in the Spirit. *'Though one may be overpowered, two can defend themselves. A cord of three strands is not quickly broken,'* (Ecclesiastes 4:12). Praying together can provide spiritual cover, and also breakthrough.

Fasting

Another tool for breakthrough is fasting. Fasting is an excellent weapon for spiritual breakthrough. It can be compared to a power drill that is used to break through the dry ground when looking for water. Jesus fasted for forty days in the desert while He contended with the enemy. Fasting was one of His weapons (Luke 4:14). Jesus probably fasted more times than was recorded, since it was between Him and the Father.

Fasting enables us to overcome the desires of our flesh, as our flesh yields to the spirit. It is a time when we abstain from the desires that feed our flesh. Instead, we feed our spirit by hungering for more of God's presence. It becomes easier to enter His presence when we surrender our flesh (body and soul) to Him. As we yield our hearts to Him, this fine tunes our spirit to hear Him more clearly. Not only that, but fasting enables God's power to work through us in greater measures than before. Fasting is powerful and can bring breakthrough in our life and the lives of others.

Fasting can release a breakthrough in the area of healing and miracles. The demon that was behind the boy's epilepsy would only come out with prayer and fasting (Matthew 17:14-21).

When Daniel received a vision of a great war, he prayed and went on a partial fast for twenty-one days. During his twenty-one day fast, a battle was occurring in the heavenly realms where the archangel Michael was fighting the principality over Persia (or the 'prince' of Persia). The spiritual battle lasted twenty one days, the length of the fast, until breakthrough finally occurred (Daniel 10:2-14).

In the natural, when we fast or abstain from food, our bodies undergo a detoxification process that is actually healthy for our bodies. Therefore, if our bodies naturally undergo a detoxification and cleansing process, our spirits probably undergo the equivalent, such as a sanctification process. Fasting enables us to become sanctified vessels for God, so He may release His power and anointing for the work He has commissioned us to do.

Satanists fast to gain more demonic power for spiritual breakthrough. However, they pray and fast to see families break up, divorces take place and to bring destruction, sickness, or death to people and ministries. If they fast to gain demonic power, think how powerful it is when Christians fast to bring Kingdom breakthrough in people's lives. Fasting is a powerful tool to contend in the spirit realm for breakthroughs on earth.

I was fasting during a time when I was desperate for breakthrough. Negative thoughts kept bombarding my mind and emotions. Then it was as if a veil had been removed where God allowed me to see things from His perspective. I suddenly saw how the enemy had been attacking my mind with these negative oppressive thoughts, all because he feared what God had in store for me. I saw how pathetic they really were compared to God's truth and promises. The moment I gave them no more attention, they simply left. This had been a battle in my mind that I finally rose above once God's truth was revealed. Breakthrough was imminent and I simply needed to hang on by ignoring the lies of the enemy. Instead, I chose to give God thanks and praise for the breakthrough that was coming.

Thanksgiving and Praise

When we give God thanks and praise by focusing on His greatness and majesty instead of our problems, I believe He releases His angels to warfare on our behalf. When king Jehoshaphat saw the vast army that was coming against him, he proclaimed a fast for Judah, and inquired of the Lord what to do. He prayed: *'For we have no power to face this vast army that is attacking us. We do not know what to do, but our eyes are upon You'* (2 Chronicles 20:12). The Lord replied: *'Do not be afraid or discouraged by this vast army. For the battle isn't yours but Gods. Take up your positions; stand firm and see the deliverance the Lord will give you'* (2 Chronicles 20:15).

When king Jehoshaphat realised the Lord was with him and would fight for them, he started to give Him thanks and praise. He appointed the worshippers to go ahead of the army. *'As they began to sing and praise, the Lord set ambushes against the men of Ammon and Moab and Mount Seir who were invading Judah, and they were defeated'* (2 Chronicles 20:22).

There may come a point after contending for breakthrough when the Lord tells us to give Him thanks and praise, even though we haven't yet seen the results. Spiritual breakthrough has to take place in the heavenly realms before we can see it take place on earth.

When we choose to give Him thanks and praise, we are rejecting the negative thoughts or fears from the enemy. Instead we choose to set our eyes on God, seeing from His perspective and through our eyes of faith. Thanksgiving and praise release faith, as we choose to focus our eyes on God instead of the enemy.

Wait on the Lord

One of the hardest things to do when contending for breakthrough is to wait on the Lord. The enemy will try every tactic to distract us, by reasoning with our minds to go and 'do something.' However, God may be telling us to wait on Him and not rush ahead. Breakthrough may happen in His perfect timing.

It is so easy to get distracted by other things or do things through our own strength and abilities. This is because we become impatient towards God or what He is telling us. However, God may want us to let go of our own ideas and wait on Him, so we may see His bigger scheme in our lives. To wait requires patience and perseverance, as we trust in His perfect timing.

God is outside of time, hence He knows the past, present and future. He always sees the bigger picture, whereas we can only see in part, or at a particular moment in time. He knows what will happen before we do. He can see the battles taking place in the heavenly realms and knows exactly what to do and when to do it. He has already seen the end results. That's why we can put our trust in Him and wait on Him. This waiting can be compared to the time when an army needs to 'camp' before they receive further instructions to advance.

David knew what it meant to wait on the Lord. He didn't give into his own man made ideas, but learnt to wait on the Lord's timing. When we choose to wait on the Lord, we are yielding our reins of control to Him. We are trusting in His timing and outcome, instead of trying to bring it about ourselves. Even though David had enemies, he still waited for the Lord's command. *'Wait for the Lord; be strong and take heart and wait for the Lord,'* (Psalm 27:14).

Whenever we choose to wait on the Lord, we are surrendering to His will and timing. Waiting on the Lord includes learning to move in the power of His Spirit through being completely dependent on God's Spirit. God is omnipotent, omniscient and omnipresent: all powerful, all knowing and everywhere. Hence, it may be wise to wait on the Lord and be led by His Spirit, especially if we want to see breakthrough.

Accessing the Courts of Heaven

In other situations, it may be right to approach the *Courts of Heaven* when seeking a breakthrough. Just as we have law courts on earth, so there are spiritual Courts in heaven. Hence, breakthrough may occur when we bring our 'case' to the Courts of Heaven. I have some prophetic friends that asked the Lord why their prayers weren't answered or they had seen no response, and the Lord told them to bring their case before His Courts. Once they dealt with their case in the Heavenly Courts, a verdict was decreed in their favour and breakthrough was seen on earth.

A pastor called Robert Henderson had been seeking the Lord and asking Him for a breakthrough in his son's life, when the Lord told him to bring the issues to the Courts of Heaven. After he did and addressed the areas of unconfessed sin, a breakthrough was seen.[1] [2]

Scripture is full of references about the Courts of Heaven, both in the Old and New Testament. Job presented his 'case' before God so he could be vindicated (Job 13:18). David commented: *'In the council of the holy ones God is greatly feared,'* (Psalm 89:7). Isaiah prophesied: *'"Present your case" says the Lord. "Set forth your arguments" says Jacob's king,'* (Isaiah 41:21).

Daniel had a vision where he saw the Ancient of Days seated at the throne, in the Courts of Heaven: *'The court was seated and the books were open,'* (Daniel 7:9-10). Satan was waging war against the saints until the Ancient of Days came and pronounced judgment in favour of the saints. Once the verdict was declared in their favour in the Courts of Heaven, breakthrough occurred and victory was seen in the battleground on earth (Daniel 7:22-26).

When John was taken up to the throne, he saw in the Spirit how the saints of God overcame the enemy: *'For the Accuser of our brothers, who accuses them before our God day and night, has been hurled down. They overcame him by the blood of the Lamb and the word of their testimony'* (Revelation 12:11). I believe John is referring to the Courts of Heaven, where satan is seen as the accuser or prosecutor. Hence, the saints won their case and overcame the spiritual battle, through the blood of the Lamb and the word of their testimony. To give a testimony means to testify, or bear witness, as occurs in a courtroom setting.

Jesus is our Advocate or Defence, and John was the disciple who referred to Jesus in this manner. *'But if anybody does sin, we have one who speaks to the Father in our defence – Jesus Christ, the Righteous One* (1 John 2:1, NIV). The same verse in the NLT says: *'But if anyone does sin, we have an **advocate who pleads our case** before the Father. He is Jesus Christ, the One who is truly righteous.'*

Unconfessed Sin

However, one of the things preventing us seeing breakthrough is unconfessed sin. In the Old Testament, battles weren't won if there was sin in the camp (Joshua 7:11-13). Only when the sin was removed, then the battle was won. Knowing this truth, David prayed; *'Search me, O God, and know my heart; test me and know my anxious thoughts. See if there is any offensive way in me, and lead me in the way everlasting,'* (Psalm 139:23).

Hence, in order to see breakthrough, we can ask the Lord if there is any 'unconfessed' sin that the enemy is legally holding against us. He will reveal what the accuser is holding against us and once we humbly address this sin, through repentance, God can decree a verdict in our favour. Once the verdict is given, then breakthrough can occur.

The enemy is known as the accuser of the brethren (Zechariah 3:1, Revelation 12:10). He prowls around looking for a legal excuse to accuse us before God our Judge. This happened to Job where satan looked for sin in Job's heart (Job 1:6-10). Things went from bad to worse until Job presented his 'case' before God his Judge. *'Now that I have prepared my case, I know I will be vindicated. Can anyone bring charges against me?'* (Job 13:18). Once a verdict was given in his favour, everything changed and Job received a double portion of blessings in return (Job 42:10).

The good news is we have Jesus who is our Advocate. He is ready to forgive all confessed sins, including the sins of our forefathers (1 John 2:1). Hence, we overcome by the blood of the Lamb. Once these sins are finally dealt with, the enemy has no legal access to accuse us before our heavenly Judge. God can now declare the legal case 'acquitted' or 'dismissed'. We are now in a position to see breakthrough as we take victory on the battlefield.

So, the reason prayers aren't answered may be because there are legal blockages. Paul tells us not to give the enemy a legal foothold through unconfessed sin (Ephesians 4:26-27). If there is something that is legally binding, then it may need to be annulled in the Courts of Heaven in order to see breakthrough on earth. It may be a breakthrough in finances, ministry, or health. Sometimes, an issue may have various layers, and when the final layer is addressed, breakthrough is seen.

Ask God for Justice

Also, we can present our case before God our Judge when seeking a breakthrough for justice. This was the case in the parable of the widow who sought justice from the judge (Luke 18:1-8). Here, Jesus was teaching His disciples about the Courts of Heaven when He encouraged them to persist in prayer.

The story was about a widow who kept bringing her case before an ungodly judge until she got the justice she deserved. It was a case to see justice brought against her accuser. She requested, *'Grant me justice and protect me against my oppressor,'* (TPT Luke 18:3). She pleaded with the judge until he finally granted her justice.

Jesus is encouraging us to approach God our Judge in the Courts of Heaven when seeking justice and breakthrough, and to persist in prayer until it is granted. This may apply when we are seeking a breakthrough with regards to relationships, finances, ministry, or healing. Instead of us giving up where there seems no response to prayer, we can bring our 'case' before God our Judge.

Also, note that she didn't come against her accuser, but brought the issue directly to the judge. She didn't have the power or authority to overthrow her accuser and humbly knew this. However, she knew someone who did have the power and authority, hence persisted until she got it.

Hence, the best place to seek justice is to go directly to our Judge. The enemy can no longer attack, steal or destroy when he is overthrown by God's decree and final verdict on an issue.

Spiritual battles can be seen as legal cases in the heavenly realms. In order to overcome, we can approach God our Judge. Jesus' final comment about the widow and the judge was this: *'And will not God bring about **justice** to His chosen ones who cry out to Him day and night? Will He keep putting them off? I tell you, He will see that they get justice, **and quickly'*** (Luke 18:1-7). Things will happen quickly on earth when God our Judge releases a decree or verdict in the Courts of Heaven on our behalf.

Repent of any Ungodly Covenants

Sometimes, there may be illegal trade deals or ungodly covenants that are preventing a breakthrough from occurring, and these can be presented before God our Judge in the heavenly Courts. In the same way things are annulled in the courts on earth, so things can be annulled in the Courts of Heaven.

When God's people had entered into a covenant with death, He made righteousness and justice the measuring line and said: *'Your covenant with death will be annulled; your agreement with the grave will not stand'* (Isaiah 28:18). I believe Isaiah was referring to a legal case in the heavenly Courts where ungodly covenants with the enemy were annulled through God's forgiveness and mercy.

Hence, each time we repent of any ungodly covenants or trade deals, before God our Judge, we can ask Jesus for His forgiveness through the power of His blood. Then God our Judge can annul each covenant through the blood of Jesus, and breakthrough may then occur.

Remind God of His Promises and Spoken Word

Other times, we may approach the Courts to remind God of His promises and purposes. What has been written in the books of Heaven concerning God's purposes for ourselves or others? What are the prophetic words we have received, or the words God has spoken regarding His calling and purposes that are yet to be fulfilled?

We can ask God for specific things to be fulfilled, according to what is written in His word and His promises. We can say, 'Lord, Your word says...' or 'Lord, Your word promises...' or 'Lord, I was given the prophetic word by 'X', that You will...' or 'Lord, You told me that You have called me to...' and so on. If we know our God-given purpose and His promised words for us, then we can present our case on the basis of this. We can ask God to let what is written in the books of Heaven concerning our present or future purposes come to pass.

Or we can ask for God to reveal what is blocking His purposes being fulfilled, and deal with this accordingly. Likewise, we can pray for others, so God's word or promise can come to pass, based on His calling and purpose for them.

Hence, we can approach the Courts of Heaven to ask God if there is anything that is being held against us that is preventing breakthrough. In His love and mercy, He will reveal the areas that the enemy is holding against us. We can repent where appropriate and forgive where needed, and then ask Jesus for His forgiveness through the power of His blood. Once the outstanding issues are dealt with, we can ask God our Judge for His verdict, and breakthrough may then occur.

'Let us then approach the throne of grace with confidence, so that we may receive mercy and find grace to help us in our time of need' (Hebrews 4:16).

Angel of Breakthrough or 'Breaker Anointing'

In some cases, we may ask God to release the *Angel of Breakthrough* to break through the enemy's camp and lead us into victory. God may anoint various people with the *breaker anointing*. This means He has assigned the Angel of Breakthrough to assist them on their God given assignments. These will be specific assignments where the Lord will release breakthrough in specific people groups or nations.

David was one of God's men who carried the breaker anointing. He only went to fight in battle if he knew the assignment was from the Lord. If the Lord wasn't with him, he refused to go to fight. However, if God was with Him, he knew there would be victory.

*'David enquired of the Lord, "Shall I go and attack the Philistines? Will You hand them over to me?" The Lord answered, "Go, for I will surely hand the Philistines over to you." So David went to Baal Perazim, and there he defeated them. He said, "As **waters break out, the Lord has broken out against my enemies before me."** So that place was called Baal Perazim,'* (2 Samuel 5:20). The Hebrew meaning of Baal Perazim is the *'Lord who breaks out'*.

When the Lord promised to deliver Israel from the hands of the enemy, He said: **'One who breaks open the way will go up before them; they will break through the gate and go out. The King will pass through before them, the Lord at their head,'** (Micah 2:13).

God is the God of breakthrough. Hence, as long as we have no outstanding sin that the enemy can legally use against us, then we can go forth and overturn the enemy's camp. Then we will see victory in our lives or the lives of those for whom we are contending, on earth as has been decreed in the Courts of Heaven.

Lord Jesus, I lay before You the areas in my life or the lives of others, where I have been praying and seen little response. Show me what to do to see breakthrough, whether I'm to contend through fasting, to wait, to claim Your word and promises, or to bring the cases before the Courts of Heaven. Lord, I'm desperate to see breakthrough and need You to show me what to do. Thank you Lord that You respond to the hearts of Your people.

END NOTES

[1] Robert Henderson; *Operating in the Courts of Heaven,* (2014)

[2] Robert Henderson; *Receive Healing from the Courts of heaven,* (2018)

Fire in the Desert

8

Growing In Grace

Grow in the grace and knowledge of our Lord and Saviour, Jesus Christ

2 Peter 3:18

One of the things we discover in the desert is *grace*. Grace is a divine enablement to fulfil God's purpose. The Lord wants us to experience the power of grace, and also how to *grow* in grace. This is because His grace is a necessity to prevent us from falling.

A self-focused life and prideful attitude prevents us from growing in grace. Hence, the Lord may call us aside and take us along a path of brokenness, until our hearts become humbled. This is why He gives His grace to the humble, because it requires a humble heart to discover and walk in the power of grace.

For most of my life I had struggled to understand the true meaning of grace. I knew about grace in my head but hadn't yet grasped the revelation of it in my heart. I finally received it in my heart when God humbled me, during a season of brokenness.

One day, as I was worshipping God whilst taking a walk, a word flashed in my mind. It was *'Grace'*. I sensed God was giving me an important key to unlock doors and prevent me from falling. Right then, I knew in my spirit this was the secret to living in His Spirit. He said, *'It is by My Grace'*. During the next few days I researched the meaning of grace in the scriptures, and asked the Lord to teach me more. I suddenly realised it was only through grace that I could be and do in Him all I was supposed to. I was no longer to rely on my own abilities or strengths, for this was simply not good enough to do the work He was calling me to.

Each day as I asked Him for grace, I was choosing to lean on His supernatural strength and power. I realised how I needed His grace when speaking or teaching, or when travelling or living with others, or when ministering. Everything requires grace! If not, then it means we are leaning on our own abilities and strength, and this may cause us to fall as a result of pride.

What is Grace?

So what is grace? Grace is a divine enablement to fulfil God's plans and purpose in our lives. It is His supernatural ability and power to do what we cannot do in the natural. This doesn't just apply to our weaknesses but also to our strengths. Hence, He will call us to do what we are unable to do, so we will learn to totally depend on Him. His grace is not just to help us in our weakness, but when we are feeling strong, because our strength is like that of a mouse compared to His strength. Grace is powerful. It provides us with the supernatural strength and energy to fulfil our calling, as we choose to follow His will.

Paul said this to Timothy: *'You then, my son, be strong in the grace that is in Christ Jesus'* (2 Timothy 2:1). During Jesus' thirty years of preparation, He grew in spiritual strength because the *grace* of

God was upon Him (Luke 2:40). Peter's last words in his letters were: '*But **grow in the grace** and knowledge of our Lord and Saviour Jesus Christ,*' (2 Peter 3:18). We are not only to grow in His knowledge but also in His grace.

God's unconditional love allows us to be saved by the power of grace. Grace is when He gives us what we do not deserve. How do we receive the gifts and anointing of the Spirit? It is through God's grace.

God opposes the proud but gives grace and strength to the humble. True humility is the awareness of our need for God, with the understanding that we can't do His work in our own strength, but only by abiding in Him.

Hence, Jesus said: '*Remain in Me and I will remain in you. No branch can bear fruit by itself. Neither can you bear fruit unless you remain in Me. If a man remains in Me and I in him, he will bear much fruit; **apart from Me you can do nothing**'* (John 15:4-5).

Humility is never self-focused or comparing ourselves to others. That is false humility. Humility is realising we need God's grace to accomplish what He has called us to do, and we can do nothing without His Spirit at work in us. Grace enables us to fulfil His commandment, 'love your neighbour as yourself', especially when we don't want to.

His grace enables us to humbly receive and become more like Him. We can receive His Spirit of wisdom, knowledge, understanding, counsel and power...through grace. God will not give His seven-fold Spirit to the proud, ambitious or self-focused (Isaiah 11:2). Rather, He will give it to those whom He inhabits. Any hidden motives such as pride, selfish-ambition, or greed, will simply block us receiving from Him. Hence, grace is required to position our hearts to receive.

The humble-hearted will recognize that it is divine grace that empowers and divine grace that enables us to have heavenly encounters and taste the powers of the age to come (Hebrews 6:5).

Jesus grew in strength for great grace was upon Him. It had nothing to do with His natural abilities. John the Beloved, was the one who referred to Jesus as being full of grace and truth (John 1:14-17). Everything Jesus did was full of grace. That is, He was completely dependent on His Father to empower Him for whatever He did or came up against. Grace is a fruit of the Spirit that is sown and nurtured in a humble heart.

Likewise, it is through divine grace that we can fulfil our calling on earth. If we rely on our own strength, it will let us down. Everything we do requires His grace, for our flesh is inadequate for the tasks ahead. This is why humility is essential to receive His grace, for without grace we will not be able to access all He has in store for us. Our own strengths and abilities will limit us or hold us back from what we can do in His Kingdom. If we want to receive the abundance He has for us in His Kingdom, then this means letting go of our natural abilities in order to receive His supernatural abilities.

Flesh Battling with Spirit

Our flesh is at constant war with our spirit, and it is our flesh that will make us fall. Hence, our spirit is to rise above our flesh. The ways we overcome is by daily surrendering our flesh to God and by receiving His grace in exchange.

Jesus said if we want to follow Him, then we must take up our cross. To follow Him is all about daily surrendering our flesh to Him, and enabling our spirit to be led by His Spirit.

As I meditated on God's grace and asked for more understanding, He gave me a picture. In the picture, I saw a person's natural strength. This person had strong, bulging muscles throughout their body, which the Lord said was their natural strength or flesh. Next, I saw them standing before Jesus and surrendering each part of their flesh to Him. Their natural strength diminished as they lay down the various parts of their carnal nature. Each part of their surrendered flesh became transformed into what looked like a tool. I saw each tool representing a part of their carnal nature such as, the need to strive, or to seek reward or be successful, or the need to lead, to defend, to compete, to take control, to criticise, to gossip, to be heard, to be accepted, and so forth.

As each piece of flesh or tool was laid down, the size of the body began to diminish until it became miniscule, like the size of a mouse. This was the result of the flesh, bit by bit, being crucified. Next, I saw the Spirit of God come and make His home in this small body. Suddenly, the body began to increase in size as the Spirit took over and inhabited it. It became far larger than the natural body. It was huge, for it was full of God's Spirit. It was full of His grace, love, mercy, kindness, peace, generosity, gentleness and so on. Then I heard these words: *'It is no longer I who live, but Christ who lives in me'*. This is because Christ can only live in the areas of our heart that we have yielded to Him.

I realised how doing things in our natural strength is simply doing things in our flesh, and it is our flesh the enemy attacks. Only when we die to our flesh can we become spiritually immune to the enemy's attacks. As we surrender the areas of our flesh to God, He will exchange them with His supernatural strength and power. This is His grace. Through His grace we can accomplish His works and overcome the power of the enemy. Someone said, 'God is moving us from human effort to spiritual muscle.'

Apostles Moving in Grace

Moses was called to be a leader but his pride and strength caused him to fall. He fled into the desert where he stayed for forty years until God called him to lead His people out of slavery. Moses, now the humblest man of God, said to God: *'Who am I, that I should go to Pharaoh and bring the Israelites out of Egypt?'* (Exodus 3:11). Moses became broken and humbled during his time in the desert, because it was the place where he died-to-self. He knew that he couldn't do what God was asking, without His grace.

The apostles moved in the power of the Spirit because *great grace* was upon them. *'And **with great power** the apostles gave witness to the resurrection of the Lord Jesus. **And great grace was upon them all**'* (Acts 4:33). The apostles understood the meaning of grace, for they could no longer operate from their natural strength or abilities to fulfil God's will. Peter emphasized the importance of growing and living by grace.

*'Each one should use whatever gift he has received to serve others, **faithfully administering God's grace in its various forms**. If anyone speaks, he should do it **as one speaking the very words of God**. If anyone serves, he should **do it with the strength God provides, so that in all things God may be praised** through Jesus Christ'* (1 Peter 4:10-11).

God is inviting us to lean on Him for our strength. When the bride came out of the desert, she was *leaning* on her Lover. She had learnt to depend on Him, no longer relying on self but now living by His grace (Song of Songs 8:5).

Rick Joyner made this comment: *'You only have true strength to the degree that you walk in the grace of God'* [1]

Jesus said: *'Lean on Me and take My yoke'*. The Message Bible describes this as His unforced rhythms of grace: *'Walk with Me and work with Me- watch how I do it.* **Learn the unforced rhythms of grace***. I won't lay anything heavy or ill-fitting on you. Keep company with Me and you'll learn to live freely and lightly'* (Matthew 11:29-30, Message Translation). We are to learn the 'unforced rhythms of grace'. This means no more striving, no more getting stressed, no more fear or holding tightly to the control reins, but learning how to freely move in His power and grace.

Paul's life was turned upside down when he saw Jesus in His power and glory. He was never going to be the same again. The old Saul had to die in order for the new Paul to come forth. He had to die to his flesh in order to grow in grace, so Christ could now dwell in Him.

'I have been crucified with Christ and I no longer live, but Christ lives in me. The life I live in the body, I live by faith in the Son of God, who loved me and gave Himself for me. ***I do not set aside the grace of God, for if righteousness could be gained through the law, then Christ died for nothing!'*** (Galatians 2:20-21).

The same verses in the Passion Translation read: *'My old identity has been crucified with the Messiah and no longer lives; for the nails of His cross crucified me with Him.* ***And now the essence of this new life is no longer mine, for the Anointed One lives His life through me- we live in union as one. My new life is empowered by the faith of the Son of God who loves me so much that He gave His life for me, and dispenses His life into mine! So that is why I don't view God's grace as something minor or peripheral.'***

When Paul let his old self be crucified, he became empowered by grace, for Christ now lived in him. Grace plays a vital part, both in the death to our flesh and our resurrection life in the Spirit. Being saved by grace is simply the beginning of this process.

Once Paul discovered this truth about grace, he said: *'I want to know Christ and **the power of His resurrection** and **the fellowship of sharing in His sufferings**'* (Philippians 3:10-11). It is the power of grace and love, that enables us to share in His sufferings. True love is sacrificial love and God gives us His divine grace to enable us to share in His sufferings.

Many Christians throughout the world have been willing to suffer for the sake of the Gospel or receive persecution for their faith. When asked, 'Would you rather be somewhere else', they commented they wouldn't exchange it for a comfortable or a safe life elsewhere, because during their times of trials and sufferings, they experienced the awesome manifest presence and resurrection glory of the Lord. His divine grace empowered them during their weaknesses, so they could rejoice, even in their sufferings.

After the apostles were arrested and flogged for speaking the name of Jesus, they rejoiced that they had been counted worthy to suffer such disgrace for His Name (Acts 5:41). How could they possibly rejoice in their sufferings? Peter gives us the answer.

*'Dear friends, do not be surprised at the painful trial you are suffering, as though something strange were happening to you. But **rejoice that you participate in the sufferings of Christ, so that you may be overjoyed when His glory is revealed**'* (1 Peter 4:12-13).

When the apostle Stephen was about to be stoned for his testimony of Jesus, he experienced the resurrection power and glory. *'But Stephen, full of the Holy Spirit, looked up to heaven and saw the glory of God, and Jesus standing at the right hand of God. "Look",* he said, *"I see heaven open and the Son of Man standing at the right hand of the God"* (Acts 7:55).

The beautiful thing is when we are willing to suffer for Him, we experience His glory-presence as well as His amazing grace. The suffering we face has no comparison to the experience of His manifest presence.

During Paul's trials, the Lord gave him divine grace. He said: '**My grace is sufficient for you, for My power is made perfect in weakness**' (2 Corinthians 12:9). Paul's response was: '*I will boast all more gladly about my weaknesses, so that **Christ's power may rest on me**. That is why for Christ's sake, **I delight in weaknesses, in insults, in hardships, in persecutions, in difficulties. For when I am weak, then I am strong.**'*

Whenever we face hardships, insults or persecutions, He gives us His grace and power to help us through. His grace gives us the inner strength to do what we naturally can't do and will empower us in our human weakness.

One week, when I was feeling unusually tired for no apparent reason, I asked God to give me His supernatural energy. As I was praying, I was reminded of what He had taught. My weary flesh was to come under the influence of my spirit, and my spirit to submit to the influence of God's Spirit. As I did this, I was leaning on God, for His power and strength in my everyday life. This was grace. But there was more to it. By leaning on His Spirit, I was also entering His rest. From now on, I was to respond to the promptings of His Spirit, instead of the promptings of my flesh. In order to do this, I had to yield my flesh to Him.

As we lean on Him, by surrendering our minds and hearts to Him, we will discover what it means to live by grace.

Lord Jesus, I ask You to reveal to my heart the meaning of grace and how to grow in grace. Teach me how to live by Your grace in all things, as I lean on You for my strength instead of relying on my flesh.

END NOTES

[1] Rick Joyner: *The Final Quest; p 55 (Whitaker House)*

9

Promotion in the Wilderness

Jesus, full of the Holy Spirit, was led by the Spirit in the desert…
He returned to Galilee in the power of the Spirit

Luke 4:1+14

There is a reason behind each desert season we encounter, and I believe God will reveal these reasons when we turn to Him and ask. However, whatever the reason, desert seasons are opportunities for God to speak to us and direct our paths.

Reasons for Being in the Wilderness

Here are some reasons we may find ourselves in the desert or wilderness.

Not in God's Will

One of the reasons we may find ourselves in the desert may be because we are not following God's will. My first experience of this was during my gap year before medical school. What I had originally planned for my gap year didn't turn out as I expected,

Fire in the Desert

and this made me turn away from God. I became disappointed with God such that I decided to get on with life by myself. However, during the following few months I felt empty and depressed. I even questioned what was the meaning of life? It felt like I was in a desert, all alone with nothing around me and nothing to see ahead.

My friends encouraged me to do a Discipleship Training School with Youth With A Mission (Y.W.A.M). Since God miraculously opened a door for this to happen, I ended up doing a three month D.T.S. During the D.T.S a pastor sensed a block in my relationship with God and encouraged me to be open with Him about how I felt. Tears welled up as I walked outside to talk with God. As I vented my feelings I cried and asked why He had left me? Why He had let me down? After releasing my emotions, I lay on my back in a field and closed my eyes.

Suddenly, a brilliant white light, brighter than the natural sun, came and overshadowed me. Then I felt God's awesome presence all around me and heard these words, *'Ange, I didn't leave you. You left Me!'* I was convicted by His words of truth spoken in such love that I instantly repented for rebelling. It was then that I realised my previous plans were never part of God's will and the reason for the gap year was to do this D.T.S. If I had known this at the beginning, then I probably wouldn't have taken the year out, since the D.T.S only lasted three months. However, what I gained in these three months was well worth the whole year out, for it transformed my relationship with God.

My wilderness season had been self-inflicted. I had walked away from God under the misunderstanding that He had let me down because things didn't work out as I hoped they would. The moment I repented, I was back in my relationship with Him and back on the path from where I left Him. My depression instantly lifted as His joy and love filled my heart. Psalm twenty three flowed out of my heart. *'He makes me lie down in green pastures, and He restores my soul.'*

We may find ourselves in the desert as a result of making wrong choices or by believing the deception that He has left us. One thing I learnt was this truth: He never leaves or deserts us (Joshua 1:5). Rather, we are the ones who leave Him.

Disappointment is the result of our *dis-appointment* with God. This means our thoughts or choices haven't been in 'appointment' or alignment with His will. Thankfully, He waits for us to return to Him just like the father who eagerly waited for the prodigal son to come back to him (Luke 15:11-32).

Drift Away From Him

Another reason we may find ourselves in the desert is when we drift away from God because we have neglected our relationship with Him. Instead, we have allowed the influences of others or distractions in this world to get in the way. We may have allowed work, ministry, finances, social media, TV, relationships, or other things to take priority, not realising our hearts have drifted from Him.

During such times we may feel 'spiritually dry' because we struggle to connect with God, or find time to be alone with Him. At times like these, I have found that it has helped when I've gone to friends for prayer, or decided to spend more time with God, for example, by going on a retreat, or by fasting from the 'distractions'. At one point in my life, the Lord asked me to fast from watching television and films, and to spend my evenings with Him. As a result, my heart and spirit grew closer to Him.

Jesus reminded us that though we are in the world we are not of this world, for we belong to Him (John 15:19). We can simply repent of the things we have allowed to come between us and God, as we choose to turn our hearts back to Him.

Fear, Angst or Stress

Another reason for entering the desert is when we allow anxiety, fear or stress to take over, or come between us and God. Most of us have probably entertained anxious or fearful thoughts more than we have listened to His Spirit. However, He wants us to include Him in every detail of our lives. He knows what is going to happen before we do, but He usually doesn't interfere unless we turn to Him or seek His will.

It is not that God isn't with us during these situations, but rather we shut Him out by allowing our fears and stresses to get in the way. Instead, He wants us to give Him our fears, stresses, and negative thoughts, and in exchange hear what His Spirit wants to say. As we yield to Him, He will take away our stresses and fears, and in exchange give us His peace.

'*The Lord is near.* **Do not be anxious about anything**, *but in everything, by prayer and petition,* **with thanksgiving, present your requests to God.** *And* **the peace of God,** *which transcends all understanding, will* **guard your hearts and minds** *in Christ Jesus,*' (Philippians 4:6-7). The peace of God will guard our hearts and minds, as we give each anxious thought to Him.

Testing of the Heart

During other seasons, we may be right in God's will and haven't veered from His path, but His presence has somehow lifted from us. I have discovered that when we feel less of His presence He can still speak to our spirit, because He is fine tuning our spirit to hear Him.

During these seasons, God is right with us even though we can't *feel* His presence, because He is testing our hearts. The moment I realised this, I would ask Him to show me what He was testing in my heart. Once I had addressed this area in my heart, I was able to engage in His presence again.

These dry seasons are opportunities for spiritual growth. He wants us to pursue Him until we find Him. He said: *'You will seek Me and find Me **when you seek Me with all your heart**'* (Deuteronomy 4:29, Jeremiah 29:13).

What I learnt one day while on the mission field in Africa I will never forget. For a few months, I had been seeking Him each morning in prayer but not feeling His presence. I had continued in faith by reading His word and through worship, but felt He was somehow holding Himself back from me. Then a fellow missionary came to my house for a coffee. This friend was sensitive to the Spirit of God and could easily sense things in the spirit realm. The moment she stepped in through my front door she said, 'Wow!' She stopped talking and was in awe of something she could tangibly sense all around her. Her eyes lit up as she looked around my room. She exclaimed, 'You have been praying much!' I asked her what she meant and how she knew.

She said the first thing that hit her as she placed her foot in my room was the tangible presence of God. I couldn't believe what she was saying. How could she feel His presence and I couldn't? I then realised the truth. He was right there with me in my room but was withholding His presence a millimetre or so from me.

He had been testing my faith and obedience to seek Him and worship Him, even when I didn't 'feel' anything. It was such an eye opener for me when she shared this. It was as if God was winking at me saying He had been there all the time just seeing how much I would press on into Him and how hungry I was for Him.

I realised how true it is that He never leaves us or forsakes us. So even if I don't feel His amazing presence, as long as I haven't erred or strayed from His path, I know by faith that He is right with me.

During such times of testing, God is stretching our faith in Him. He does this because He wants to see if we really do love Him. Do we want to know His will? Do we trust Him? Will we wait for Him? He is actually right with us even if we can't feel Him. Hence, we can persevere in faith as we keep our hearts focused on Him.

Faith doesn't rely on our feelings, because it is a choice we make in our spirit. I believe God will take us into a deeper relationship with Him if we are willing to press on further into Him and not give up. He wants us to seek His presence but this requires a hunger in our hearts for more of Him.

The truth is He is always with us and will never leave us or desert us. So if we haven't left Him, then that means He is with us. Hence, we can invite Christ to dwell in our hearts *through faith* (Ephesians 3:17).

Higher Calling

For some, the wilderness season is a time when God calls His bride to come and be alone with Him, so He can reveal more of Himself to her. These are God appointed seasons where He is calling us to a lifestyle of deeper communion with Him. The higher the call means the greater the cost. This is a call to a life of abandonment to Him, where we choose to abide in His presence.

This season may feel like a wilderness, where it is just you and Jesus walking together. It is the bridal price to follow Jesus, our Bridegroom-King. During such seasons, we may develop a passion for Him that burns in our hearts. There is no going back, as our life becomes hidden in Him. Our reward is that He will dwell in us as we dwell in Him.

I had just completed a mission assignment in Africa and sensed God had something new for me to do. I knew I was in a season of transition and expected doors to open for my next mission, but that didn't happen. Instead, a friend offered me to stay at her flat somewhere on the coast. Initially I said 'thank-you, but no thank-you' for I thought it was not for me. However, when I realised that God had provided her flat as a place for me to stay, I took up her offer. During the first few days, I felt alone as if I was on a desert island, because God had taken away the things that mattered in my life. These were the things that I belonged to.

During my first week as I felt alone, I asked God, 'Why was this happening?' I desperately wanted to be somewhere where I felt I belonged. Then the question came, *'Where is my belonging and what do I belong to?'* I was looking to belong to things, like a church or mission organisation or family, but God popped the answer in my head. He said: *'Ange, I don't want you to belong to anything else but to Me!'* I was so surprised. He then gave me a picture, where I saw myself with a cord around my waist that represented a yoke. This cord was more firmly yoked to my church and mission organisation, than it was to Him. He wanted to shift my mindset, so I became more yoked or bonded to Him than any other influence in my life. Hence, He had removed me from the things I had become too attached to.

In all of this, He was showing me that He wanted me to be first and foremost bonded to Him. He is to be my belonging. I am to belong to Him. Then I can be attached to other things, like a church or organisation. This is not saying we are to isolate ourselves from the body of Christ. On the contrary! We are to be a part of the body of Christ and accountable to others. However,

God wants us to be more committed or bonded to Him than we are to anyone or anything else.

During this season, the Lord revealed how I had been seeking others to meet my needs. This included the needs for approval, affirmation, recognition, to be valued, and to be listened to. God asked me if I would go to Him for all my needs. He wanted me to come to Him for approval, recognition, affirmation or to be listened to. Was He enough? Could He meet all my needs?

I decided to go on a fast because my heart wanted more of His presence. It was on the third day of the fast that His presence came and overwhelmed me. I found myself spontaneously thanking and praising Him before going to bed and on awakening each morning. It no longer bothered me that I was alone in an unfamiliar place away from everyone. I started to enjoy my time, just being with Him and no-one else. This was His doing. It then didn't bother me what I did next. I just wanted to be with Him. He had simply pulled me aside to get me away from everything that mattered to me, so He could be the only thing that now mattered. It felt like I was on a honeymoon with Him, just the two of us enjoying each other's company.

This desert experience of feeling alone and isolated soon blossomed into a wilderness with flowers. It was just me and Him, enjoying time with each other. I said one day, *'Lord, all I want now is You!'* He was waiting for me to come to this point in my relationship with Him. No longer was I bothered about what I did next or who I was with. All that mattered was that I was in union with Him. This wilderness season was God's doing, so I could become more yoked and bonded to Him.

Spiritual Pruning

Sometimes a barren season can feel like a time when nothing much seems to be happening or little fruit is seen to be produced.

However, this can be an opportunity for God to prune back our old ways of thinking and doing, so He may show us new ways in His Kingdom. Hence, the dry seasons may be a time for God to do some spiritual pruning in our hearts, so we may grow and produce more Kingdom fruit. These are moments to embrace, as we allow His Spirit to do the deeper work in our hearts.

It was during my season of transition that God revealed it was necessary for Him to do the deeper work in my heart, if I wanted to bear more fruit for Him in His Kingdom. He had much more in store for me to do, but first I had to be pruned so new shoots could grow.

Training for Reigning

Desert seasons may be a time of training for reigning. Esther had to undergo a year of preparation before she was ready to become queen. During this time she developed a mindset and heart that was pleasing to her king. However, she had to lay aside all her ambitions and plans, as she chose to serve her king and give up the rest of her life for him.

God has great plans for each one of us, like He did with Esther, but it may require a time of preparation in the wilderness, where we allow Him to refine our hearts, so we may grow deeper in our relationship with Him.

Israelites in the Wilderness

In Deuteronomy, we discover why God led His people through the desert. *'Remember how the Lord your God led you all the way into the desert these forty years, to **humble you** and to **test you** in order to **know what was in your heart**, whether or not you would keep His commands. He humbled you, causing you **to hunger** and then feeding you on manna, to teach you that man doesn't live on bread alone but on* *every word that comes from the mouth of the Lord'* (Deuteronomy 8:2-3).

Let's look at the reasons why God led the Israelites through the wilderness.

To be Humbled

The first was to *humble them* so that they would know their need of God. God may bring us to a place of brokenness in our hearts where we realise that we can't do anything without Him. One of the things He may ask us to surrender to Him is our natural abilities.

For many years I was under the false belief that my abilities were my own doing as a result of my studies, training and hard work. Then one day God revealed to me that *all* my abilities came from Him. He created me to be able to take on such abilities and opened the doors to develop them. Having this revelation made me realise that I could take no praise for myself since it was His doing all along, and not mine.

God reminded the Israelites that when all was going well in the Promised Land, they were not to let their hearts become proud or forget what He had done. *'You may say to yourself, "My power and the strength of my hands have produced this wealth for me". But remember the Lord your God, **for it is He who gives you the ability to produce wealth**'* (Deuteronomy 8:14, 17-18).

To Test their Hearts

The second reason the Israelites were in the wilderness was to *test what was in their hearts*. What were their real motives and intentions in life? Were they really after God's heart? Would they still obey Him and keep His commands, or rebel and do what they wanted? Would they hunger for Him and His Word or focus on their flesh and the things of this world? God may lead us in the desert to expose and test what is in our hearts.

The Israelites didn't pass this test of their hearts because they moaned, complained and focused more on their flesh and selfish desires, than they did on God. Hence, that generation didn't make it through the wilderness and into the Promised Land.

To see how Hungry they were for God

The third reason was to see if they were *hungry to know Him more*. Did they hunger for His Word more than they hungered for food? The Israelites moaned about what they were eating and complained that the manna from Heaven wasn't sufficient. God wanted them to cry out for more of His living bread, His heavenly word. He was trying to teach them that man doesn't live on bread alone but on every word that comes from the mouth of God (Deuteronomy 8:3). Sometimes, the Lord may lead us in a desert to simply increase our spiritual appetites for Him.

The reason the Israelites didn't make it out of the desert was because they kept failing to obey and were rebellious in their hearts. Hence, God waited forty years until the next generation were of age to make it into the Promised Land.

*'Today if you hear His voice, do not harden your hearts as you did in the **rebellion**, during the **time of testing in the desert**, where your fathers tested and tried Me and for forty years saw what I did. That is why I was angry with that generation, and I said, **"Their hearts are always going astray, and they have not known My ways"**. So I declared on oath in My anger, **they shall never enter My rest'** (Hebrews 3:7-19, Psalm 95:7-11).*

Jesus in the Desert

Jesus had to undergo a time in the desert. He was probably alone and no-one knew where He was or what He was doing except His Father, the Holy Spirit, and satan.

*'Jesus, full of the Holy Spirit, returned from the Jordan and **was led by the Spirit into the desert, where for forty days He was tempted by the devil**. He ate nothing during those days and at the end of them He was hungry'* (Luke 4:1-2).

After His baptism, Jesus was *led by the Spirit* into the desert, for this was God's will. Though He was alone, God was with Him. During His forty day fast, He was tested with His flesh, mind, will, identity, and emotions, as well as His relationship with God. Jesus experienced the same tests that the Israelites faced but He revealed that it was humanly possible to overcome each test.

Test of Identity

Jesus was tested with His identity. This was tested just after God had said to Him: *'You are My Son, whom I love; with You I am well pleased'* (Luke 3:22). The devil challenged Him and said, *'If you are the Son of God....'* Satan knew full well who Jesus was but wanted to take the opportunity to test Him on His identity.

Jesus didn't have to prove who He was to anyone. He knew who He was and that was all that mattered. So He didn't respond to this temptation, but instead chose to ignore it. As a result, He passed the test. When God teaches us things on a personal level, like our spiritual identity, we are usually tested to see if we have grasped this revelation in our hearts.

Test of Spirit versus the Flesh

Secondly, Jesus was tempted by the flesh. Satan knew He was hungry so he tempted Him to change a stone into bread and break

His fast. The weapon Jesus used to retaliate was the Word of God. He said, *'It is written: Man does not live on bread alone, but on every word that comes from the mouth of God'* (Mathew 4:4).

The Greek word used here for 'word' was *rhema* and referred to the breath of God or word breathed by the Holy Spirit. This is the sword of the Spirit (Ephesians 6:17). Hence, the words He spoke came from the mouth of God.

He was referring to the passage in Deuteronomy when the Israelites themselves were tested in the desert. The Israelites failed this test, but Jesus gave the right response and passed. He overcame the desires of His flesh by spiritually feeding on the Word of God, and therefore His spirit took mastery over His flesh.

Test of Obedience to God

Next, satan tempted Jesus by showing Him all the kingdoms of the world and saying: *'I will give You all their authority and splendour, **for it has been given to me**. So if You worship me it will all be Yours'*. Jesus' response was again to use the sword of the Spirit, the Word of God. He replied: *'It is written...'* and went on to quote the scripture: *'Worship the Lord your God and serve Him alone'* (another quote from Deuteronomy 6:13).

Jesus overcame the temptation by declaring the truth through the Word of God, and by worshipping God alone. He allowed nothing to get between Him and His Father, not even wealth, splendour, power or fame. He was totally devoted to His Father.

Test of God Given Power & Authority

Jesus was tempted a second time with His identity, but also with His authority and power. Satan cunningly quoted the scripture from Psalm 91: *'Then the devil took Him to the Holy City and had Him stand on the highest point of the temple. "If you are the Son of God", he said, "throw yourself down. For it is written: 'He will command His angels concerning you, and they will lift you up in their hands, so that you will not strike your foot against a stone,"'* (Mathew 4:6).

This demonstrated how satan twists the truth to tempt us to sin, like he did with Adam and Eve. However, Jesus replied again with the Word of God: *'It also says, "Do not put the Lord your God to the test."'*

He overcame all tests and temptations with the sword of the Spirit, that is the *rhema* word of God (Ephesians 6:17). He was tested with His flesh, pride, identity, status, power, authority, and obedience to God's will. After He had passed these tests and God was pleased with His heart, He left the desert.

Jesus was tempted in every way, just as we are, yet was without sin (Hebrews 4:15). God doesn't tempt us, though He allows our hearts to be tested.

'God is faithful; He will not let you be tempted beyond what you can bear. But when you are tempted He will also provide a way out so that you can stand up under it' (1 Corinthians 10:13). God has given us the free will to say 'no' to sin and temptation, by either ignoring it or walking away from it.

Finally, Jesus was promoted as He left the wilderness: *'Jesus returned to Galilee in the **power of the Spirit**'* (Luke 4:14). After He left the desert, Jesus received the power and anointing of the Spirit, as the Spirit came and rested upon Him. He then read from the scroll of Isaiah 61: *'The Spirit of the Lord is upon Me, because He has anointed Me...'* (Luke 4:18). Now, He was ready to step into the work that His Father had called and anointed Him to do.

Promotion in the Wilderness

These Spirit-led wilderness seasons are divine opportunities for God to lovingly transform our hearts. Hence, we will come out looking different to when we entered. Even the friends of

Solomon didn't recognise his bride when she came out of the wilderness: *'Who is this coming up from the desert leaning on her lover?'* (Song of Songs 8:5).

Joseph, Moses, David, John the Baptist and Paul, spent years in the desert. These were times when their hearts were being shaped, refined and prepared by God for their divine purposes and callings.

Joseph's desert was a prison. The prison was a place where Joseph's heart was refined and tested, as he was being spiritually prepared for the promotion that God had in store for him.

Moses was living in the desert when God appeared to him in a burning bush and commissioned him to lead His people out of Egypt and into the Promised Land (Exodus 3:1-4).

David had been fleeing from Saul and hiding in the caves and strongholds in the desert. He underwent thirteen years of training for reigning as he faced many trials and challenges where his heart was constantly tested. After his time of preparation in the wilderness, he was promoted to be the next king (1 Samuel 23:13).

John the Baptist was a man who was set apart for God. He was called to live in the wilderness, eating locusts and honey, and was the voice of one calling in the desert, to prepare the way for the Lord (Mark 1:3).

After Paul's conversion experience on the road to Damascus, he withdrew and spent the next three years in Arabia (which is thought to be around Mount Sinai) and later in Damascus (Galatians 1:17-18). This was training ground where Paul spent time alone with God, hearing Him and receiving Kingdom revelation. God was preparing Paul for his future ministry. After his three years alone with God, he joined the other apostles in their ministries.

Each of these amazing men of God had a significant time alone with Him, where God was preparing their hearts for the call that was on their lives. Their hearts were being prepared to carry the weight of responsibility that came with their anointing.

The wilderness is not just a time of testing, but also a time of spiritual promotion. What we overcome takes us to a new level in our relationship with God, and releases greater Kingdom authority. James encourages us to count it joy when we face different trials, for it is a testing of our faith: *'Blessed is the man who perseveres under trial, because when he has stood the test, he will receive the crown of life that God has promised to those that love Him'* (James 1:2-12).

Wilderness seasons don't have to be long if we discover what God is testing in our hearts, and rightly respond. Otherwise, we may end up going around in circles, having to face the same test again and again until we finally overcome.

In the world, we may have to pass a test or exam to gain the qualification that is required for a job or promotion. Likewise, God may anoint and appoint His people in His Kingdom after we have overcome certain tests of the heart. This is for our benefit as well as the benefit of others. His amazing love for us never changes, even when we fail.

Wilderness seasons can actually be times of preparation, where God is preparing our hearts for future promotions in His Kingdom. However, this requires pressing deeper in Him, and not being influenced by the distractions or temptations of the enemy. The more we allow our flesh to be crucified, the more we will discover the fullness of a resurrected life in Him.

Lord Jesus, thank You that it is Your desire to take me deeper in Your heart. Help me to see what You are doing, so I may overcome the tests of my heart, and step into Your divine will and purpose.

10

From Outer Court to Bridal Chamber

Who is this coming up from the desert leaning on her lover?

Song of Songs 8:5

The desert is the perfect place where God draws His children out of the world and into the chambers of His heart. Our hearts become transformed by His love, as He calls us to a deeper place of communion with Him.

During such seasons, we may find ourselves laying down our ambitions, agendas, careers, and even ministries, as He invites us into the chambers of His heart. As we pursue His presence, we are creating a place in our hearts where His Spirit can dwell.

He is preparing our hearts to become hosts of His presence, as we discover how to abide in Him. The things that take place in the secret place will overflow from our hearts in the public place. As someone once said, 'The secret place is the practice place for the market place.'

Tabernacle

The word 'tabernacle' was also known as the 'tent of meeting'. This is because the tabernacle during the time of Moses and Joshua was a mobile tent. It served as a temporary dwelling place to commune with God, as Moses and Joshua journeyed through the wilderness.

'Now Moses used to take a tent and pitch it outside the camp some distance away, calling it the 'tent of meeting'. Anyone inquiring of the Lord would go to the tent of meeting outside the camp,' (Exodus 33:7).

As God led the Israelites through the desert, He was teaching them how to 'tabernacle' with Him. This was through prayer, worship, and learning to move with His presence. His presence manifested as a cloud by day and fire by night. Not only that, but they could find rest in His presence. *'My Presence will go with you, and I will give you rest,'* (Exodus 33:14).

However, Jesus made a way for us to tabernacle with God through His death on the cross. Hence, we no longer need to meet Him in a man-made tabernacle, for *we* have become His tabernacle. This means He can come and tabernacle with you and me. Paul said: *'Do you not know that your body is a temple of the Holy Spirit, who is in you, whom you have received from God?'* (1 Corinthians 6:19).

When Paul spoke to the Ephesians, he was referring to Christ dwelling amongst a *corporate* body of believers: *'In Him you (plural) too are being built together to become a dwelling in which God lives by His Spirit,'* (Ephesians 2:22).

Jesus spoke these words before His death: *'If anyone loves Me, he will obey My teaching. My Father will love him, and We will come to him, and make Our home in him,'* (John 14:23). Jesus is inviting us to become tabernacles of His presence. Instead of just receiving a visitation, He is inviting us to become a habitation. The Lord wants to make His home in our hearts, so we may dwell in Him and He may dwell in us.

A temple usually had three areas, known as the *Outer Court*, *Holy Place* and *Holy of Holies*. The Holy of Holies was also known as the *Most Holy Place* or the 'chamber of all chambers'. Each represented the chambers to God's heart, since the temple is seen as the very heart of God. *'I did not see a temple in the city, because the Lord God Almighty and the Lamb is its temple'* (Revelation 21:23). The Lord wants to come and dwell in our hearts, and He is inviting us to come and dwell with Him, in His chamber of all chambers. Hence, Jesus said: *'Remain in Me and I will remain in you,'* (John 15:4).

Spirit, Soul & Body

The spirit, soul and body can be seen as representing the three parts to God's temple. This is because we are His living temple or His dwelling place. Therefore, our body can be seen as representing the Outer Court, since this is our outer part that is in contact with the world. The soul (mind, will and emotion) may be seen as representing the Holy Place. The priest would usually sanctify himself before entering the Holy Place. Likewise, we can sanctify our minds, wills and emotions, through the cleansing power of His blood, in order to engage our hearts with Him.

Finally, since the spirit is our inner dwelling, then this can be seen as representing the Holy of Holies, or the place where our spirit tabernacles with Him.

When we spend time resting in His presence and communing with His Spirit, it will have a positive effect on the soul and body. This is because what flows out from the inner sanctuary flows through the rest of the temple.

Gold, Frankincense & Myrrh

When the three kings (or wise men) visited Jesus at His birth, they came with three gifts. One brought gold, another frankincense and the other myrrh. What was the significance of these three gifts?

Myrrh was the gift of suffering-love and signified obedience unto death. Hence, it represented the cross that Jesus would have to endure.

Frankincense was one of the oils and spices burnt on the altar. It was an incense (hence the name 'frank-incense') used by the priest during the times of intercession in the temple. It produced a white smoke that may be seen as representing purity.

Gold represented wealth, riches and the glory that was seen with the kings and queens. Even the heavenly Kingdom is paved with gold. The elders have crowns made of gold and the New Jerusalem, the city of God, is made of transparent gold (Revelation 4:4, 21:18).

Hence, these three gifts can represent three attributes of Jesus' heart. Myrrh represents the heart of a *Suffering Servant*, frankincense represents the heart of a *Priest*, and gold represents the heart of a *King*. In a similar way, the Lord is nurturing our hearts, so we may carry the heart of a servant, priest and king. (More on this can be read in the book '*Into His Chambers*'[1]).

The apostle John witnessed the twenty four elders and four living creatures singing these words: '*You were slain, and with Your blood You purchased men for God from every **tribe and language and people and nation**. You have made them to be a **kingdom and priests to serve** our God, and they will **reign on the earth**,*' (Revelation 5:9-10).

The Lord is calling forth His people from every tribe, tongue, and nation, at such a time as this, to be His servants, priests and kings who will serve Him in His Kingdom, here on earth.

Esther

One day, the Lord drew my attention to the book of Esther and revealed there were three stages in Esther's life, and how each stage may be seen as representing one of the chambers in His tabernacle.

First stage

In the first stage, Esther was seen as an orphan who lived under the care of her cousin, Mordecai. This was a time when she lived in the world and probably did what most people in her culture did. This phase in her life can be seen to represent the Outer Court in the temple, because the Outer Court was the area that was in contact with the world.

Second stage

The second stage was when Esther received the invitation to the king's palace. Here, she was being set apart from the things of the world. This was her season of preparation and training for reigning. This stage may represent the Holy Place in the temple, because the Holy Place was for those who were set apart for God. It was where the priests would prepare themselves to encounter the Lord Almighty.

Third stage

The third stage was when Esther encountered the king. However, she had to wait for the king to invite her into His bridal chamber. This was seen as the chamber of all chambers, or the Holy of Holies, and represents the inner sanctuary in the temple.

Let us look at the Outer Court, Holy Place and Holy of Holies in more detail.

Outer Court

The Outer Court was usually the largest area in the man-made temple and was like a courtyard. Hence, it would have a gate surrounded by walls or fences, and was always outside the sanctuary. Most people could enter and exit this part of the temple, since it was the part that was connected to the outside world.

One of the ways people entered was by giving thanks and praise. Hence, we enter His gates with thanksgiving and His courts with praise (Psalm 100:4). The Hebrew word for 'court' is *chatser*[2] and refers to the courtyards in a temple. Hence, worship is one of the keys that can prepare our hearts to engage with God, and to enter in His presence.

The Outer Court served as a connection between the world and God. The Israelites were allowed to enter the court to worship and give offerings, but only the Levites or priests were allowed to enter into the sanctuary.

When Esther lived with her cousin, Mordecai, she probably went each week to the temple. However, she only had access to the Outer Court. She probably knew about the king but only from a distance, or from what she read or heard others report.

Holy Place

After the Outer Court was the entrance to the sanctuary. It was customary for the Levites and priests to have access to the sanctuary. The sanctuary was divided into two parts by a thick curtain or veil, that is, the inner and outer sanctuary. The outer sanctuary was known as the Holy Place, and as the name implies, it was holy ground. So those who entered were to first wash themselves and take off their shoes along with their outer garments. This was a sign of reverence and honour, as they acknowledged they were entering into God's holy presence. Likewise, it may be customary to take off our coats and shoes as a sign of respect and honour, whenever we enter someone's home or dwelling place.

In the Holy Place, there was a table with some bread, a lamp burning with oil, and an altar for burnt offerings. The altar was used on a regular basis by the priests as they made burnt offerings and sacrifices on behalf of the people and themselves.

The lamp was to burn with oil at all times. It consisted of six branches, three on each side and seven lights. Each branch had a light and the seventh light was in the centre. This lamp is known as the *menorah*. Each of the seven lights can be seen to represent the seven-fold Spirit of God (Isaiah 11:2, Revelation 4:5, Exodus 25:31). The bread was known as the bread of His Presence. By eating the bread, the priest was keeping in 'communion' with God.

The veil was thick as it divided the inner sanctuary from the outer sanctuary. However, the veil was ripped from top to bottom when Jesus gave up His last breath on the cross. Through His perfect sacrifice on the cross, we now have access by His blood, into the Holy of Holies.

'Therefore brothers, since we have confidence to enter the Most Holy Place by the blood of Jesus, by a new and living way opened for us through the curtain, that is, His body,' (Hebrews 10:20). Hence, the veil or curtain can be seen as His torn flesh.

The Holy Place is where we enter into Communion with the Lord, as we eat the bread of His Presence and drink His blood. As we do this, we are feeding on His heavenly manna, His living word, His Kingdom DNA, and receive His cleansing through the redeeming and sanctifying power of His blood. In return, we can choose to offer our body, soul and spirit to Him, as a living sacrifice, as we come to the altar of incense (Romans 12:1). The altar of incense stood on the other side of the veil, in the Holy of Holies.

The Holy Place is a place where we humbly prepare our hearts to engage with His presence, as we focus our minds on Him. It is where we ask Him to sanctify our hearts and minds through the cleansing power of His blood, so we may enter His presence.

The time may come when the Lord calls us to leave our worldly lifestyles and make our hearts a place of habitation for Him. This will look different for each one of us but it will be a call to step aside from our worldly affairs and invest more of our time in Him. It is an invitation to come in a deeper place of intimacy with Him, as we say 'yes' to follow Him.

The Lord is calling His people to serve as kings and priests in His Kingdom, but this requires yielded hearts as we willingly lay down our lives for Him (Revelation 5:10). Peter said: *'You are a chosen people, a royal priesthood, a holy nation, a people belonging to God'* (1 Peter 2:9). Peter had the revelation that those who belong to God are His royal sons and daughters. Not only this, but His royal children are called to be holy and to be priests in His Kingdom.

When Esther was taken in the palace, she was being set apart for the king. Esther's heart was to undergo a process of sanctification and transformation. It was a place of purification and preparation before she could meet the king, face to face, in the bridal chamber.

God may set us apart from the things of the world, so our hearts may tabernacle with Him. This may be a season of training for reigning, as it was in the case with Esther. For others, it may feel like being set apart from the 'normal crowds'. Instead of having our needs met by the many, we are discovering how to have our needs met by just the One.

After David was called and anointed by Samuel, he went through a desert period. This ended up being thirteen years of Kingdom schooling and preparation, before he was finally inaugurated as king.

Twelve Months of Preparation

During Esther's time in the palace, she received twelve months of 'beauty' treatment. This consisted of six months of Myrrh followed by six months of other perfumes, oils and spices. Myrrh is a well known spice mentioned throughout the scriptures. Its Hebraic meaning is 'bitter suffering' or 'suffering love'. This is because Myrrh comes from the gum of a thorny, knotted tree and when the bark is pierced it has drops looking like tears of red gum that ooze forth. Hence, Myrrh is seen as bitter suffering, as it represents the drops of blood that oozed forth when Jesus was pierced on a tree. Myrrh was also one of the three gifts presented to Jesus at His birth. This signified the suffering that was to come, as a result of His obedience unto death.

When Esther received Myrrh during her first six months of purification, it signified her obedience unto death. Her life was no longer to be her own or centred on herself, but on the king. Hence, she had to undergo a time of inner cleansing and purification as well as healing of past wounds. It was probably a time of personal grief and loss, as she underwent the process of death-to-self and transformation in her heart.

When the Lord calls us into deeper communion with Him, it may involve some personal grief. He may ask us to lay down personal things for Him, as He invites us to share in His Kingdom.

When I surrendered my life to the Lord, He asked me to lay down my medical career for Him. He made it clear that I couldn't be 'married' to my paediatric profession if I wanted to give my life to

Him. Hence, He took me through a process of personal grief, as I gave up my career and said say 'yes' to follow Him.

For many, this may seem too hard a call. Hence, many are called but few are chosen. The chosen are those who say 'yes' to God's will, no matter what the price. God gives us His amazing grace to lay down the things He asks, so we may step into the life He has called us to live with Him.

The desert, or in Esther's case it was the palace, is a time of transition and preparation, as we say 'yes' to the call to become His bride.

Holy of Holies

After the outer sanctuary is the inner sanctuary or Holy of Holies. Few were invited into the Holy of Holies because it was the place of His glory-presence. Nothing profane was allowed to enter, for it was and is the *Most Holy Place*. The high priest was the only one who could enter and this was just once a year, on the Day of Atonement, known as *Yom Kippur*.

In the Holy of Holies was the Ark of the Covenant that contained the golden jar of manna, the budding rod of Aaron, and the tablets with the commandments. Above the Ark was the mercy seat. This was the dwelling place of the glory of God. Nothing defiled could enter or touch the Ark or it would die. Hence, only the high priest could enter and before he did, it was essential that he was cleansed and sanctified. He would enter with a rope attached to his body in case he was found to be unclean. If this was the case, he would die in the Most Holy Place and be pulled out by the rope. Hence, the reverential fear of the Lord was in the hearts of those who entered the Holy of Holies.

Some may believe that the Ark of the Covenant or the Holy of Holies isn't relevant today and was a thing of the Old Testament.

However, when the apostle John was taken up to heaven, he witnessed the Ark of the Covenant: *'Then God's temple in heaven was opened, and within His temple was seen the ark of His covenant. And there came flashes of lightning, rumblings, peals of thunder, an earthquake and a great hailstorm,'* (Revelation 11:19).

When the bride-to-be declared, *'Let the King bring me into His chambers'* she was referring to a chamber within a chamber, or the Holy of Holies (Song of Songs 1:4 TPT). It is God's desire for His children to dwell with Him in His inner sanctuary, His bridal chamber. However, this comes at a price, and includes a hunger for more of His presence.

There is a sense of reverence and awe when the King of kings and Lord of lords is welcomed at gatherings or meetings, and appears in His glory-presence. When we experience His manifest presence, we are communing spirit to Spirit, heart to heart, and it is the most glorious of moments or places to be. This is His bridal chamber, the place where we commune with Him, in His glorious presence.

Finally, the time came when Esther was to be ushered into the king's chamber. After having twelve months of purification and beauty treatment, she was ready to meet the king, face to face, in the bridal chamber.

The Holy of Holies is the glory chamber, the place where the bride meets her Bridegroom King, and the two become one. As a result of Jesus' death on the cross, He made it possible for us to lift up the veil and see Him face to face, in His inner sanctuary, the place where His glory dwells.

When the bride meets the bridegroom, she lifts up her veil, so she may see him and become one with him. *'And we, all with unveiled faces who reflect the Lord's glory, are being transformed into His likeness with ever-increasing glory'* (2 Corinthians 3:18).

Before Jesus faced the cross, He prayed this prayer to His Father, that we may be one with Him, as He is with the Father: *'I pray that all of them may be one, Father, just as You are in Me and I am in You. I **have given them the glory that You gave Me, that they may be one as we are one: I in them and You in Me,**'* (John 17:21-23).

The bridal chamber is a place where holiness and reverence are tangibly felt before the throne of the King. Jesus provided a way for us to enter the very heart of God, through His torn flesh and blood (Hebrews 10:19-20).

In the supernatural realm, the Holy of Holies is huge. It is not a small place as is seen in the natural tabernacle. It is like walking through enormous doors that we are invited through. This is because it is His throne room (Ezekiel 43:7) and the place where His seven Spirits abide (Isaiah 11:2, Revelation 4:5). Hence, we can welcome the seven Spirits of Wisdom, Revelation, Knowledge, Fear of the Lord, Counsel, Power, and His Presence, as we engage with Him, in His Holy of Holies.

Heart of the Bride

'Behold, I'm standing at the door, knocking. If your heart is open to hear My voice and you open the door within, I will come into you and feast with you and you will feast with Me,' (TPT Revelation 3:20).

When Jesus spoke these words to the Laodicea church, He was inviting the lukewarm-hearted people to become His bride. The Passion Translation comments on this verse as follows:

'Jesus knocking on the door points us to the process of an ancient Jewish wedding invitation. In the days of Jesus, a bridegroom and his father would come to the door of the bride-to-be carrying the betrothal cup of wine and the bride-price. Standing outside, they would knock. If she fully opened the door, she was saying, "Yes, I will be your bride." Jesus and

His Father, in the same way, are knocking on the doors of our hearts, inviting us to be the bride of Christ.'

In the Song of Songs, the king discloses the characteristics and qualities of his bride. Here are some qualities mentioned in the Passion Translation. (I have highlighted the characteristics in bold.)

*'You are **true royalty**! The way you **walk so gracefully in My ways** displays such dignity. Out of your **innermost being is flowing the fullness of My Spirit**- never failing to satisfy. Within your womb there is a birthing of harvest wheat; they are **the sons and daughters nurtured by the purity you impart**. How **gracious you have become**! Your life **stands tall** as a tower, like **a shining light** on a hill. Your **revelation eyes are pure**, like pools of refreshing- sparkling light for a multitude. Such **discernment surrounds you**, protecting you from the enemy's advance. **Redeeming love crowns** you as royalty. **Your thoughts are full of life, wisdom and virtue**. You **stand in victory** above the rest, stately and secure as you **share with me your vineyard of love**,'* (TPT Song of Songs 7:1-7).

Royal Behaviour - *'You are true royalty...redeeming love crowns you as royalty'*

One of the qualities of the bride is her royal behaviour because she knows her royal identity. During the first years of life, we usually know little about our identity. The same can apply when we are 'spiritual toddlers' in the body of Christ. However, as we continue to grow and mature in the Spirit, we will come to understand our spiritual identity and what it means to be royal sons and daughters of the King. The closer we come to Jesus, we will not only see Him as our Brother, Lord, and Saviour, but also as our Bridegroom-King.

Though we are in the world, we are not of the world, because we belong to another Kingdom. God is nurturing our royal identity as

He prepares our hearts to be His bride, so we may reign with Him in His Kingdom.

Walking in God's Ways with Grace - *'The way you walk so gracefully in My ways displays such dignity'*

One of the priceless attributes of the bride is the ability to walk in grace. When the bride came out of the desert, she was leaning on her lover (Song of Songs 8:5). This was a posture signifying her intimacy with the King. As we continue to grow in our royal identity, we will discover how to grow in grace. Grace is given to the humble and flows from a place of intimacy with Him. It is true that what we worship, we become. Hence, we begin to grow more in His grace, the more we spend time abiding in His presence.

Carry the Fullness of His Spirit - *'Out of your innermost being flows the fullness of My Spirit'*

As the bride continues to grow and mature in her relationship with the King, she will discover the fullness of sonship in Him. Spiritual growth is a process where we gradually mature from born-again babies to immature sons to mature sons and finally to become His bride.

There will come a point in our spiritual growth when the Lord will invite us to enter an extravagant life of abiding in His presence. As we engage in this lifestyle with Him, we will discover the fullness of sonship, as the Spirit of the Lord takes full residence in our hearts (Isaiah 11:2).

Nurturing Spiritual Sons & Daughters – *'Within your womb is a birthing of harvest wheat: they are the sons and daughters nurtured....'*

As the bride reaches a place of maturity in her heart, as is seen in her relationship with the King, she will become a spiritual mother to many. This is when she births new things in the Spirit that the

Lord gives her to nurture, and this includes nurturing God's sons and daughters into their fullness of sonship.

In the book of Revelation we see the bride clothed with the brilliance of the sun, giving birth to a man-child or mature son. The bride was led into the wilderness where she was protected and nourished by God for three and a half years. Her spiritual offspring are those who overcome by the blood of the Lamb and the word of His testimony, as they willingly lay down their lives to serve the Bridegroom-King (see Revelation 12).

Purity & Integrity of Heart – *'Your revelation eyes are pure'*

One of the beautiful aspects of the bride is her pure, transparent heart. This is seen in her eyes since the eyes are the gateway to the soul. With purity comes revelatory insight, and that's why the pure in heart will see God (Matthew 5:8). The bride stands out from amongst the crowd because she radiates such inner beauty. She walks fully covered in the armour of light, as she abides in His presence (Psalm 91).

Carrier of Wisdom & Discernment – *'Such discernment surrounds you...your thoughts are full of life, wisdom and virtue'*

As the bride grows in spiritual discernment, she learns to discern the things that are from the world, flesh, and devil, and the things that are from God. She has learnt to listen to His Wisdom instead of the wisdom of the world (1 Corinthians 1:30). Instead of following fear, she chooses to follow Him. Hence, she carries Wisdom and discernment as a result of following the heart of her King.

Stands in Victory – *'You stand in victory above the rest'*

The bride discovers how to overcome the ways of the enemy and stand in a place of victory with her Bridegroom-King (Ephesians 6:17). She is aware of her power and authority, and carries it with such grace and humility. Her battles are fought with King Jesus, as she obeys His divine commands and follows His strategies. She is one who overcomes by the blood of the Lamb, and the word of her testimony, by giving her life as a sacrificial love-offering to her Bridegroom-King (Revelation 12:11).

Jesus Prepares a Place for Us

Before Jesus died on the cross, He said these profound words to His disciples: *'In My Father's house are many rooms; if it were not so, I would have told you. I am going there* **to prepare a place for you.** *And if I go and prepare a place for you,* **I will come back and take you to be with Me'** (John 14:2-3).

The Greek word used here for 'rooms' is *'Mone'*[3] and means 'dwelling place,' 'place of rest,' or 'abode'. It means more than a physical place because Jesus uses this same word a few verses later. *'If anyone loves Me, he will obey My teaching. My Father will love him and we will come to him and make our home [Mone] with him,'* (John 14:23).

Jesus was referring to making His home our home by Him coming to dwell in us. We are His living temples. He will no longer dwell in a physical building or temple but in our spiritual bodies. However, one crucial thing had to take place before this was made possible. Jesus had to go to the cross to tear down the veil. Hence, we now have access through His blood, to enter into the sanctuary of His glory-presence, the place of divine rest where we come into union with Him.

Jesus said He will not only prepare a place, but He will come back and take us to be with Him. The Greek word used for 'come back and take' is *'Paralambano'*[4] and it is the word used when referring to taking a wife or coming back for the bride. It is an intimate act of taking, as if taking unto oneself. Jesus was speaking to His disciples about us dwelling in intimate union with Him and the Father, because He was coming back for His bride.

He is calling us to this life of abiding in His presence. It is a bridal level of intimacy where we simply live our lives abandoned to Him. All we do flows from a place of extravagant worship and intimacy with Him. And in return, His glory-presence comes and dwells in us.

Lord Jesus, help us to pursue Your presence so we may enter into Your chamber of all chambers. Give us a greater revelation of the chambers of Your heart, so we may dwell in You and You in us.

END NOTES

[1] Dr Walker, Angela; *Into His Chambers, 'Four Faces' (Chapter 12)*

[2] Chatser (Hebrew 2691); *Strong's Expansive Exhaustive Concordance: Red Letter Edition*

[3] Mone (Greek 3438); *Strong's Expansive Exhaustive Concordance: Red Letter Edition*

[4] Paralambano (Greek 3880); *Strong's Exhaustive Expansive Concordance: Red Letter Edition*

Fire in the Desert

11

His Burning Ones

*Love is as strong as death, its jealousy unyielding as the grave.
It burns like blazing fire, like a mighty flame*

Song of Songs 7:6

The Song of Songs is an amazing book and allegory of our betrothal and marriage to King Jesus. At the beginning, the *bride-to-be* asks the king to bring her into His chamber of all chambers (Song of Songs 1:4). In her journey with the king she encounters joy, romance, suffering love and the desert. Finally, it is the *bride* who comes out of the desert, and she is leaning on her lover (Song of Songs 8:5). Interestingly, the spice known as Myrrh is mentioned more times in the book of Song of Songs than any other book in the Bible, and refers to suffering love.

At the end, the Bridegroom-King speaks these words to His bride: *'Fasten me upon your heart as a seal of fire forevermore. This living, consuming flame will seal you as my prisoner of love. My passion is stronger than the chains of death and the grave, all consuming as the very flashes of fire from the burning heart of God. Place this fierce, unrelenting fire over your entire being'* (TPT Song of Songs 8:6).

The bride is consumed with the fire from the heart of God, as her heart becomes sealed with His flames of love.

One day, the Lord showed me a huge fire with flames that were over ten feet tall. This fire was made of an outer and inner ring. The outer ring was made of red flames that surrounded an inner ring of golden flames. Around the fire were two groups of people: those who stood warming their hands, and those who chose to walk through the flames. Then I heard these words, 'Fire falls on sacrifice'. The people who were warming their hands were like onlookers, who wanted to receive the heat but were not prepared to encounter the flames. The outer red ring was like a consuming fire. However, you had to pass through the consuming flames before you could encounter the golden flames - the fire of His glory.

I believe this was an invitation for us to walk through His fire and offer ourselves to Him as a living sacrifice (Romans 12:1-2). Hence, His fire always falls on sacrifice (1 Kings 18:38). His fire consumes our hearts as we fully yield ourselves to Him (Hebrews 12:29). After we have encountered the consuming flames, we will be invited into the golden flames - the fire of His magnificent glory-presence.

The prophet Zechariah describes something similar. *'And I Myself will be a wall of fire around it,' declares the Lord, 'and I will be its glory within,'* (Zechariah 2:5).

Who are His Burning Ones?

The Lord is preparing our hearts to become carriers of His fire and glory. He is preparing new wineskins to contain the new wine of His Spirit. He no longer wants us to follow religion or man-made theology, but instead to follow His Spirit. Then our hearts will beat in tune and rhythm with His heartbeat, as our spirits become one with His. Once our hearts have been consumed by His fiery-passionate love, then our lives become no longer our own, but His.

Here are some of the treasures that may be found in the hearts of His burning ones.

Abiding in His Presence

One of the treasures found in the hearts of His burning ones is a hunger for His presence, where the heart becomes a resting place for Him.

Many times I have read this verse: *'This is the word of the Lord to Zerubbabel: "Not by might, nor by power, but by My Spirit", says the Lord Almighty'* (Zechariah 4:6), but didn't see how it was linked to the previous verse. In the previous verse the angel showed Zechariah a gold lamp-stand with seven lights and a bowl on top. When the angel spoke these words to Zechariah, 'Not by might...' he was referring to these seven lights on the gold lamp-stand (Zechariah 4:2-6). What are these seven lights? He refers to them as being the eyes of the Lord. *'These seven are the eyes of the Lord which range throughout the earth'* (Zechariah 4:10).

If we fast forward to the book of Revelation, we see that the seven lamps and the seven eyes are actually the seven Spirits of God. *'Before the throne, seven lamps were blazing. These are the seven spirits of God'* (Revelation 4:5). *'Then I saw a Lamb, looking as if He had been slain, standing in the centre of the throne. He had seven horns and seven eyes, which are the seven spirits'* (Revelation 5:6).

What does all this mean? If we read the book of Isaiah, it says what the seven Spirits are. *'The **Spirit of the Lord will rest** on Him- the **Spirit of Wisdom** and of **Understanding**, the **Spirit of Counsel*** *and **of Power**, the **Spirit of Knowledge** and of the **Fear of the Lord**'* (Isaiah 11:2).

These are more than the gifts referred to in 1 Corinthians 12, because a gift is a miniscule portion of the Spirit. The gifts of wisdom and knowledge are described as a *word* of knowledge and a *word* of wisdom (1 Corinthians 12:8). This is tiny compared to the actual *Spirit* of wisdom and the *Spirit* of knowledge. Jesus didn't operate from the gifts of the Spirit for He was God incarnate, the Word made flesh. Hence, the Spirit of the Lord was in and upon Him.

When the angel said to Zechariah, 'Not by might but by My Spirit', he was actually referring to the seven Spirits of God coming and resting on us. This is referring to a lifestyle of abiding in His presence. It is when we abide in Him that we encounter His Spirit of Wisdom and Understanding, Counsel and Power, Knowledge and the Fear of the Lord. I believe this is referring to the fullness of Christ dwelling in us, as we learn to become hosts of His presence.

The Lord is calling us to co-labour *with* Him. Many of us are doing things *for* Him when He may be asking us to do things *with* Him. He is preparing our hearts to say 'yes' to Him and to follow Him, whatever the cost. He is calling us to *be* with Him, dance *with* Him, laugh *with* Him, share in His suffering love, and abide *in* Him. He longs to share His manifest presence, but first we are to remain in Him, so He may remain in us (John 15).

As we choose to abide in His presence, our lamps are being continually filled with the oil of His Spirit. This is because the oil that is required to keep the virgin's lamps burning is the oil of His presence (Matthew 25:1-13). Hence, as our hearts continue to host His presence they will keep burning with His fiery love.

Waiting on the Lord

Another treasure in the hearts of His burning ones is the willingness to wait on the Lord and seek His face. Some may fast and pray, as they wait for His manifest presence.

God is never in a rush and enjoys it when we walk with Him at His pace, instead of our own. Most of us rush off and do things our way with our own plans and agendas, while God is waiting for us to come to Him and seek His strategy from a place of worship and surrender. He is calling us to be Marys, not Marthas. He has amazing things to reveal to our spirit, but this requires waiting on Him and giving our time to Him. He will come and overshadow us, as we wait on Him and surrender our time to Him.

Jesus waited for thirty years before receiving His mantle of anointing. After His resurrection, He told His disciples to *wait* in Jerusalem for the promise His Father would give to them (Acts 1:4). The Greek word used for wait is *'Perimeno'* [1] and means to wait regardless of what is going on around us. That means not to get caught up in our circumstances or other agendas, but make God our main focus.

As the disciples waited on God, they met together and constantly prayed (Acts 1:14). They didn't allow themselves to become pre-occupied with other things, but just worshipped, as they eagerly waited for Him.

I happened to be out walking whilst on a retreat, when the Lord told me to stop rushing ahead but to walk at His pace, that is, if I wanted to hear Him and be with Him. So, I slowed down my pace and literally stopped when I felt Him stop and walked when I felt His Spirit was moving. It was a spiritual exercise to discover how to walk step by step with Him, and in doing so, remain in His presence. We can hear Him as we learn to walk with Him and wait on Him, and hence respond to the moves of His Spirit.

When Moses went up to the mountain to hear the Lord, he waited for six days before the Lord spoke to him (Exodus 24:16). David knew what it meant to wait on the Lord (Psalm 130:5, 27:14). Waiting on the Lord is something we have lost in the body of Christ, for we want quick fixes to everything. Yet those who patiently wait for the Lord will go deeper in their communion with Him. It is when we wait on the Lord, that we have fresh revelations, supernatural encounters, and life transforming experiences.

It is during the times when God seems silent, that we are to pursue His presence and not give up. During these times of 'waiting', He is fine tuning our spirit. Instead of relying on our common sense, logic or man-made suggestions, He is fine tuning our spirit to hear Him.

I happened to be walking on a beach, when I saw a surfer get on his board and swim out in the ocean. Next, he turned around to position himself on his board to ride a wave. However, he had to wait for the right wave to come at the right time. I continued to watch, and after a period of waiting, I saw the right wave was about to come. He was rightly positioned as he waited for the right wave. Then as the wave came it lifted him high and took him to the shore.

God is wooing us to come into the ocean of His presence and to wait on Him, as we rest in His presence. He is calling us to watch and pray, so we are ready to ride on the waves of His Spirit. As we rest in His presence, He is preparing our hearts for the next moves of His Spirit. He will release the right waves at the right time in the power of His Spirit, as we wait on Him.

The secret to moving in the power of His Spirit is to rest in the ocean of His presence. *'Those who wait on the Lord will renew their strength. They will soar on wings like eagles; they will run and not grow weary'* (Isaiah 40:31). His ways and timings are not ours, but they are perfect.

The late Jill Austin said this about waiting on the Lord; *'Waiting kills our flesh and it purifies our motives. Waiting is never a waste of time because God is always working out what we are waiting for. His timetable is not like ours. Forty years is not a long time in God's mind. For us, with our microwave mentality, forty minutes is a very long time. We want it in thirty seconds. We call it delay; God calls it perfect timing. We call is slow; God calls it just right. Training for reigning is a prophetic journey, a dramatic saga that lasts a lifetime.'* [2]

Waiting is a lost art for few are willing to spend time waiting on God. We live in a world governed by time and are driven by success and achievement. Hence, we want instant fixes to our problems and believe it is all about 'doing'. Some may believe that prayer or waiting on God is a waste of time, yet it is the secret to going deeper with Him and living in His presence. He is calling His sons and daughters to come into the ocean of His presence so we may ride with Him, on the waves of His Spirit.

Moses and David knew that unless God's presence went with them, it simply wasn't worth it, for there would be consequences. Hence, they only moved forth *if* His presence went with them. Moses stayed put unless the cloud moved by day or the fire by night. Likewise, David enquired of the Lord if he was to fight in a battle (2 Samuel 5:19). Both Moses and David reached such a depth of friendship with God that they were willing to wait on Him until He responded.

Are we willing to wait on God, not just fifteen minutes or an hour, but as long as it takes to encounter His presence? God is looking for people who will seek Him and not give up. He is looking for people who are committed to Him instead of the things of this world.

The prophet Hosea wrote: *'After two days He will revive us; on the* **third day He will restore us, so that we may live in His presence.** *Let us acknowledge the Lord;* **let us press on to acknowledge Him,'** (Hosea 6:2-3). Let us be those who are willing to spend time waiting on Him, as we abide in His presence.

Laying Down our Lives

Another treasure in the hearts of His burning ones is the willingness to lay down their lives for Him. Jesus gives us the grace to lay down our lives for Him, as He invites us to follow Him. One of the first things God asked when He called me to the mission field was to lay down my medical career. He was inviting me to sacrifice my life for Him, just as He had sacrificed His life for me.

When we co-labour with God, He gives us the grace to serve, to reach out to others, to love, to minister, to listen to people, and to do all the things we don't want to do. Hence, grace enables us to move in His Spirit instead of defaulting to our flesh.

Jesus gives us the grace to die to our flesh or 'self' so we may follow Him. *'If anyone would come after Me, he must deny himself and take up his cross daily'* (Luke 9:23). Whenever I have looked into the eyes of Jesus I have seen such meekness and love that is beyond words. His meekness and love melts my heart, bringing tears to my eyes. I am instantly humbled and undone as I look into His eyes of sacrificial love, and my heart can only say 'yes'. The Lord will lovingly ask if we are willing to sacrifice our lives for Him, so our life is no longer our own, but His. Let us receive His sacrificial love in our hearts, and in return, offer ourselves as a living sacrifice for Him.

Unity of the Spirit

Another treasure in the hearts of His burning ones is the unity of the Spirit. God is calling His sons and daughters to be united in His Spirit, because we need one another to do the work our Father has called us to do. This includes standing and covering each other in prayer. His anointing flows in greater measures whenever there is true unity in the Spirit (Psalm 133:1-2). God loves us co-labouring with Him, as we minister together in the unity of His Spirit.

One way we can maintain a spirit of unity is by coming together at His table to share in His body and His blood. There have been countless times when I have felt led to take Communion with fellow believers, and during such moments, He has released His love and unity amongst the team.

One of David's qualities was to fight for unity. When his men were quarrelling, complaining, or even accusing him, he sought the Lord. He chose to listen to God instead of man, and in doing so, he restored unity amongst his men.

Unity of the Spirit is essential in God's End-Time army, so we may move in His power and anointing, and overcome the works of the enemy. His burning ones choose to honour one another, as they see each other through the eyes and heart of God. His power and anointing falls on His burning ones as they remain united to His Spirit.

'Be completely humble and gentle; be patient, bearing with one another in love. Make every effort to keep the unity of the Spirit through the bond of peace' (Ephesians 4:2-3).

Let us make every effort to keep the unity of the Spirit, by loving one another as ourselves.

Purity

Another attribute of His burning ones is purity in heart. David said: *'Who may ascend the hill of the Lord. Who may stand in His holy place? He who has clean hands and a pure heart'* (Psalm 24:3-4).

One of the things the Lord lovingly does is to purify our hearts. As we go through His fires, He will draw to the surface any hidden motives, selfish-ambitions, agendas, or things of the flesh, so our hearts may become pure and transparent. Our sins can be readily forgiven and our hearts made pure, through the sanctifying power of His blood (1 John 1:9).

After David committed adultery with Bathsheba, he prayed these words: *'Wash away all my inequity and cleanse me from my sin. Cleanse me with hyssop, and I will be clean; wash me and I will be whiter than snow.* ***Create in me a pure heart, O God, and renew a steadfast spirit within me,****'* (Psalm 51: 2+7+10). Jesus is coming for the bride who has prepared her heart for Him (Ephesians 5:26-27, Revelation 19:7). Let our hearts be ready for the Bridegroom-King.

Radical Obedience & Faith

Another treasure is that of radical faith and obedience to His will (Galatians 3:11, Romans 6:16). Jesus' disciples lived a life of radical faith as they followed and obeyed Him to the end (James 2:14-26).

His burning ones live by faith and not by sight, as they seek first His Kingdom instead of the things of the world (Matthew 6:33). Faith is a choice in our spirit that is to rise above our fears and emotions.

One day, the Lord revealed to my spirit that He has given us two feet: one is faith and the other is obedience. In order to step out in faith with one foot means we have to step out in obedience with the other. Hence, faith and obedience work together, because you can't have one without the other. Let us be those who step out in radical faith and obedience to His Spirit (James 2:18-26).

Seek their Reward from God

Another treasure in the hearts of his burning ones is complete dependency on the Father. His burning ones no longer seek their reward from man or the things of the world, because they have chosen to seek their rewards from the King.

Many may be functioning from an orphan heart when striving after success, or seeking rewards from man. His burning ones no longer strive for success as the world does, but seek their rewards from Him (Luke 10:20). All our financial needs, emotional needs, and spiritual needs are met by Him. This includes the need for affirmation, the need for acceptance, the need for recognition, and the need to be loved. Our identity is not in what we do or who we know on earth, but comes from our relationship with King Jesus and the Father.

Ezekiel tells the beautiful story of an orphan baby that was adopted by God. God took this baby into His care and nurtured her, and she became His little princess. As she continued to grow and mature, she reached an age when she was ready to enter a covenantal relationship with Him. So He covered her with the corner of His robe and made a covenant with her, and she became His. Finally, He gave her a crown and anointed her as queen. Her fame spread as a result of her royal beauty and divine splendour. However, it wasn't long until her downfall came, because she chose to put her fame and splendour before her Bridegroom-King.

She prostituted that which had been given her, by using it for her own gain and glory (Ezekiel 16:1-15).

Jesus resisted fame and fortune. He never looked for attention or a platform. Those He healed He instructed to tell no-one, except the priest. He didn't seek publicity or the lime light or charge any fees for His ministry, but He freely gave to all. He lived by faith, knowing His Father would provide. Jesus chose to obey His Father's will and give Him the glory. He sought nothing for Himself, not even a home or possessions, not even a wife. When the Israelites wanted Him to be king, He fled. His reward was with His Father, for His Kingdom was not of this world.

God is looking for those whom He can trust with His glory. He is looking for hearts that seek nothing from this world, not even fame, fortune, a platform, or promotion, but instead choose the way of the cross. He is looking for those who are willing to sacrifice their lives for Him.

'Do not rejoice that the spirits submit to you, but rejoice that your names are written in Heaven' (Luke 10:20). Let us be those who seek our rewards from Him.

Fear of the Lord and a Sanctified Life

One of the main differences between Saul and David was that Saul feared men whereas David feared the Lord. This cost Saul his anointing, whereas David was promoted. His burning ones not only revere His name but pursue a sanctified lifestyle. David knew what it was to love God with all his heart and seek His face, but he also feared His awesome power and holiness. His relationship with God mattered more than anything else. He was so conscious of God's holiness and awesome power, that he never wanted to grieve Him.

Isaiah was undone when he encountered the Holy One, the King of kings and Lord Almighty, seated on the throne. He fell facedown to the ground full of reverential fear (Isaiah 6:1-8). Nothing can withstand the most holy, almighty, all powerful, thunderous and glorious presence of God. Once we encounter the reverential fear of the Lord, we are changed forever.

Let us be those who reverentially fear the Lord and pursue a sanctified lifestyle, as our hearts burn with His fiery-love.

Lord Jesus, take me through Your consuming flames of love and put a seal on my heart. Transform my heart with Your fiery love, as I yield all of myself to You. Set my heart on fire and increase my hunger for more of Your presence, as I daily follow You.

END NOTES

[1] Perimeno (Greek 4037): *Strong's Expanded Exhausted Concordance: Red Letter Edition*

[2] Jill Austin; *Dancing With Destiny;* p48 (Chosen 2007)

Fire in the Desert

13

Tabernacles of His Glory

*I have given them the glory that You gave Me,
that they may be one as We are One: I in them and You in Me*

John 17:22-23

Throughout the scriptures, God gives special attention to His holy temple. When the Israelites were in exile in Babylon, the hand of the Lord came upon Ezekiel and he was taken in the Spirit to a high mountain. On this mountain, he saw a city and within this city he was taken to the new temple.

Ezekiel was shown the features of this temple, including the inner and outer sanctuary. He heard the voice of the Lord like the roar of rushing waters as the glory of the Lord filled the temple. The temple was to become His dwelling place. The Lord continued and told Ezekiel to look carefully and listen closely, paying special attention to what He was about to tell him regarding the temple.

He said: '*Give attention to the **entrance of the temple and all the exits of the sanctuary**...no foreigner **uncircumcised in heart** and flesh is to enter My sanctuary*' (Ezekiel 44:4-9). The entrances and exits were to be guarded, so nothing profane was allowed to enter God's holy sanctuary.

The same may be seen to apply to His *living* temples. Since we are His living temples, this means to guard what we allow in, by filtering what we see and hear, and be careful of what we allow out, through filtering what we think or speak. Hence, this passage may also refer to the guarding of our hearts and minds, so that His Spirit may come and dwell in us.

If we fast forward to the Book of Revelations, we will find something similar. When the apostle John saw the Holy City, the New Jerusalem, coming down from heaven, he saw it as the bride fully prepared for her husband. He heard these words from the throne:

'I saw the Holy City, the new Jerusalem, coming down out of Heaven from God, prepared as a bride beautifully dressed for her husband. And I heard a loud voice from the throne saying, "Now the dwelling of God is with men and He will live with them. They will be His people, and God Himself will be with them and be their God"' (Revelations 21:1-3.)

The beautiful thing is, there is no temple in the city because the Lord God Almighty and the Lamb *are* the temple. Also, the city doesn't need the sun or moon to shine, for the glory of God gives it light, and the Lamb is the light (Revelation 21:22-23). Nothing impure is allowed to enter but only those whose names are written in the Lamb's Book of Life.

Encounter His Glory-Presence

In the Old Testament, there were certain regulations that the priests had to follow as they entered the sanctuary. Essentially, they had to prepare themselves by washing their hands and putting on clean garments. Though these were physical requirements, they had spiritual meanings.

In a similar way, we can spiritually prepare our hearts as we engage with God, so we may encounter His glory-presence.

One of the ways to come spiritually prepared is by cleansing the entrances and exits to our hearts. These are like our 'gateways' and each gateway can be cleansed through the sanctifying power of His blood. So what are the entrances and exits to our hearts?

We have five natural senses and these can be seen as our gates or entrances. The five senses include our sight, hearing, smell, taste, and touch. These are also our spiritual senses. Hence, we can ask the Lord to cleanse our senses, so we may see, hear, smell (or discern), taste (or speak) and feel (or sense) in the Spirit, as we engage in His presence.

Likewise, we can ask the Lord to cleanse the gateways to our soul, by sanctifying our mind, will, emotions and imagination. This is so we may 'think', 'feel' and 'imagine' things in the Spirit, and be discerners of His 'will', as we open our hearts to engage with Him.

As we cleanse our gateways, we are preparing our hearts to encounter His presence. Some may feel the desire to posture themselves by lying or kneeling on the ground, and others may lift up their hands before the Lord. Hence, our hearts and spirits can engage with Him, as we surrender ourselves to Him.

We can enter the place of divine rest as we engage in His presence. Some may breathe-in His Spirit as they welcome Him in their hearts by faith (Ephesians 3:17). Some may encounter Him through the eyes of their hearts, or with their sanctified minds or imaginations, or simply by resting in His presence (Matthew 13:15). We can enter this place of rest through grace (Hebrews 4:16). There comes a time when it becomes easier to engage in His presence, once we have created a place in our hearts for Him to dwell.

Ocean of His Presence

A few years ago, I was attending a prayer meeting when I had a vision. In the vision, the Lord was calling His people to come into the ocean of His presence. From this place of rest in the ocean of His presence, I saw four things happen.

First, I saw a person *walk on water* and had the words 'radical faith'. The person didn't allow their surrounding circumstances to pull them down, but they walked in the midst of storms by simply keeping their eyes focused on Jesus.

Second, I saw a person standing on the water and looking far out over the horizon. They were able to see from a distance what was coming, and hence prepare the rest of the body to get ready. These were the watchmen – the prophetic men and women in the body of Christ, who keep watch as they abide in the ocean of His presence.

Third, I saw a person diving deep in the ocean to discover the hidden treasures and pearls of wisdom. These represented the hidden mysteries and revelations in the Kingdom for us to discover, as we dive deeper in His presence. Others were invited to explore these hidden mysteries and revelations, by seeking the Spirit and going deeper.

And fourth, I saw a person being carried on the waves as they moved under the power and anointing of the Spirit. There were miracles and healings, as God's power was displayed wherever they went. They were moving under the fresh anointing and outpouring of His Spirit, as their spirit came in alignment with His Spirit.

All of these four 'movements' were not by might or by strength but by the power of His Spirit, and each was birthed from the place of resting in the ocean of His presence.

There was *radical faith* to do the outrageous and impossible. There were *hidden revelations* concerning truths and mysteries, as a result of going deeper in His presence. There were *prophetic watchmen* to prepare the body for what was coming and prepare the way for the Lord. And lastly, the waves of *anointing* for those who aligned themselves with the new moves of His Spirit, to minister healing, miracles, and transform lives wherever the Spirit sent them.

I believe this vision represents the life we are called to live, but occurs when we rest in the ocean of His presence. Whatever we do in His Kingdom is to be birthed from the place of abiding in Him.

A prophetic friend gave me this word: *'Don't be concerned with what you will be doing, it is all about what you are becoming (being). If you seek Him for the transformation in you, then whatever you are doing, wherever He takes you, the Kingdom will come through you.*

Even if you are doing the right thing, if you should fall into thinking that doing the right thing is the key, then you will be using the wrong key!

The right key is what you are being. God has been working on your character as that is key. He is making you into a doorway to link heaven and earth (opened by the key of what you are being), then the Kingdom will come wherever you are.

What you are doing will flow from what you are being! Once you have found a place of rest in who you are in Him, where you go and what you do can flow from this.'

This confirmed that what we do is to flow from our hearts, as we pursue a lifestyle of resting in His presence.

Soaking In His Presence

Soaking in His presence is a phrase that simply means taking time to be still with God and rest in His presence. In the same way we may take a bath to soak our bodies, so we may take a 'spiritual soak' by focusing our hearts and minds on Him.

This is a time when people may choose to lie down or simply rest, as they engage in His presence. Some may prefer to play some worship music, whereas others may enjoy the silence. As we take time to be with Him, we can welcome His presence to be with us.

It is creating time to be still before Him, since true worship is an act of our surrender to God. This is an opportunity for us to wind down and just focus on Jesus. Some may say words like, 'Come, Lord Jesus,' and others may give Him thanks or praise.

Benefits of Soaking

There can be various benefits when we soak in His presence and here are some of them.

Marinate

There are some benefits when we soak or allow ourselves to marinate in His presence. When raw food is placed in marinating ingredients, the longer it is left to soak, the more taste and colour it absorbs. Likewise, the more we soak in His presence, different flavours or aromas may start to exude from our hearts. *'For as a man thinks within himself, so is he'* (Proverbs 23:7). Or to put it another way, what we worship, we become.

Likewise, an unwashed cooking pot usually requires soaking in warm water, to soften the hardened areas. In a similar way, God may soften the hardened areas in our hearts as we soak in His presence. Soaking can allow the Holy Spirit to reach deep down in our hearts, where ordinary prayer may not reach.

People have testified to healing, simply through soaking in His presence. God loves it when we hang out with Him, as it allows Him to do deeper work in our hearts.

Abiding in Him

There was a man called Brother Lawrence who learned how to practice the presence of God in his daily routine life. He engaged with God in everything he did and not just the times he spent in the chapel. His simple lifestyle of communing with God has become known as *'Practicing the Presence of God'*. [1]

As we spend time soaking on a regular basis with the Lord, we will become more aware of His presence in our daily life. Jesus said if we remain in Him, He will remain in us (John 15:4). This remaining refers to spending time abiding with Him. It is the same when a man and woman spend time in each other's company. The more time they spend together, the closer they become, as they become aware of each other's presence.

At the beginning of the year, I felt prompted by God's Spirit to spend my evenings soaking in His presence. So I decided to do this for a season. An hour or so before I went to bed, I would put on some worship music and turn my attentions to Him. At the beginning, I gained little from each evening and wondered if it was worth continuing. However, I decided to continue, for I was doing it for Him. Gradually, I started to feel His presence engage with me each evening.

A few weeks later, I became aware of His presence during the day. Suddenly, I would sense His presence around me as I was doing something routine. It was beautiful, as I realised He was returning His love to me, for the evenings I had given to Him. Hence, when we draw closer to Him, He draws closer to us (James 4:8).

Prepare for Tsunami Waves

Many times, I see the ocean is like His presence and the waves are like the moves of His Spirit. A surfer has to wait in the depths of the ocean if they want to ride the big waves. The further we go out in the depths of His presence, the greater are the waves we will ride.

Some years ago, the Lord spoke about riding on the waves of His Spirit, where I saw three types of waves. There were small waves, medium waves and tsunami waves. Most people were seen to be surfing on the small waves, for these were easy to ride and there were minimal risks involved. Then there were some who were surfing on the medium size waves. These were the people who were prepared to go further out of their depth, and hence they were willing to take more risks as they did.

Then there was the third wave and this was called the 'death wave'. There were very few surfing this wave because it was a tsunami wave, and this required a complete 'death-to-self'. A person had to be willing to lay down their life before they could ride this wave. The reason for this was because their flesh (fear, pride, ambition, control, and so on) would pull them under the waves. Hence, it required a complete death-to-self in order to ride this wave, because their focus was to be completely on the Lord. I realised that the deeper we go, the greater the cost, but the greater the waves we will ride with Him in the Spirit.

A natural tsunami occurs after there has been a violent shaking that causes the water to be displaced from the sea-bed. The shaking usually occurs as a result of a natural disaster, such as, an earthquake or volcano. In a similar way, the Lord may release His 'spiritual tsunamis' after the 'spiritual shakings' in the body of Christ. The Lord is preparing our hearts to ride these waves with Him, the deeper we are prepared to go in the ocean of His presence.

Accessing His Glory-Presence

It is one thing to minister with the gifts of the Spirit, and another to minister under the anointing of the Spirit. However, there is another way to minister to others, and this is through ushering in His glory-presence.

Whenever we minister under an anointing, the anointing power will flow through us and out to others. This can feel exhilarating when it happens, though we may feel tired or exhausted afterwards. However, when we usher in His glory-presence, then everyone can get to encounter His presence, and instead of feeling tired, we feel energised.

This is because our spirit becomes supernaturally charged the more we rest in His presence. In the same way a mobile phone becomes charged when it is plugged into a live socket, so we become supernaturally charged as we plug our spirit into the live socket of His Spirit.

A dry sponge is designed to absorb water. However, more water starts to leak out of the sponge the more it is left to soak. Likewise, the longer we rest in Him, the more we will overflow as we begin to 'leak out' His loving presence.

Spending our time with Him is a key to becoming a carrier of His presence. Hence, learning how to be a carrier of His presence in the secret place enables us to be an usher of His presence in the public place. Each time we usher in His glory-presence allows others to personally encounter Him. Some may laugh, cry, shake, fall, or simply enjoy being in His presence. However, instead of feeling tired, we may find ourselves energised or super-charged. This is because our spirit becomes charged whenever we rest in His glory-presence.

In a vision, I saw myself worshipping with a tribe of people in a remote African village. Then it was time for me to deliver the message. However, at this point, the Lord asked me to take a step back and welcome Him into the meeting. So I stepped back and welcomed Him in, by ushering in His presence. Nearly everyone fell on the ground as they responded to His manifest presence. Some were laughing and crying, and others were radically healed and set free as they each encountered His presence. I didn't lay a finger on anyone, but was laughing in the Spirit myself, as I witnessed this happen in the vision. I realised that when we usher in His presence, it means we can step back and allow Him to do whatever He wants at a meeting.

There was a small group of six guests from the USA who visited an Iris mission base to minister to the staff and the mission school students. During one of the meetings, the six guests decided to form what is known as a 'fire tunnel' for the staff. A fire tunnel is created when people stand in two rows facing each other with their hands lifted high to create a tunnel for others to walk through. As people walk through the tunnel, those forming the tunnel usually pray for God's Spirit to fall and for His fire to come.

It so happened that these six guests had been soaking in the Spirit for some hours before they came to the staff meeting. They appeared 'drunk in the Spirit' as they were laughing and swaying. This fire tunnel was the smallest I have ever been through, since it only consisted of six people, where there were just three standing on either side. However, it was the most powerful one I have encountered.

Two metres before I even reached the guests, I was hit by God's Spirit and overwhelmed with His presence, such that I started to laugh and felt wobbly on my feet. I fell to the ground and crawled my way through the tiny fire tunnel and lay flat on my back once through the other side. I was undone with His joy as I laughed in the Spirit and enjoyed being in His presence.

These six guests were overflowing with His Spirit because they had been soaking in His presence. As they ushered in His presence, the staff fell on the ground as God ministered to every missionary. It was a beautiful and unforgettable moment, when God's glory-presence crashed on the missionaries through the six guests who knew how to usher in His presence.

I believe the Lord is preparing our hearts to be those who usher in His glory-presence at gatherings, so He may come and take over the meetings, doing far greater things than we can ever do.

Chariots of Fire & Glory

I would like to finish with something Heidi Baker shared in one of her visitations with the Lord. In this powerful encounter, she was taken up to heaven and suspended above the earth where she saw surrounding the globe thousands upon thousands of chariots of fire, carrying the glory of the Lord. Inside each chariot were two saints of God and they were totally transparent. There was nothing hidden in them, no darkness, nothing disguised, and they were full of glory and full of light. The only colour she saw was a huge red heart that went from shoulder to shoulder, beating with passion. Each heart of the saints of God was beating in rhythm with the heartbeat of Jesus.

Then the Lord said to Heidi: *'Tell the church, release control! I will hold the rein to this revival. I will decide where the chariots run. Tell the church- release the reins to Me!'* Then she saw the Lord's right hand above His head, and His hand went down as He cried *'Now!!!!!'* And the chariots of fire and glory began to run across the face of the earth, and fire, glory-fire, fell upon the earth. Then she asked these questions: *'Who would ride in the chariots of glory? Who would carry the huge heart of Jesus' love within them? Who would ride the chariots of glory and not touch or rob the glory? Who would release control to the Bridegroom–King?'* [2]

His glory chamber is the place of habitation, where we commune heart to heart, spirit to Spirit, with His divine presence. He is looking for a bride who will become a tabernacle for His presence, a carrier of His fire and glory. The invitation is there for you and me, to enter into the chamber of all chambers of the Bridegroom-King.

Lord Jesus, I give You the control reins in my life as I choose to live for You. Change me, heal me, transform me, deliver me, as I give my life as a love offering to You. Lord Jesus, take me into Your chamber of all chambers, so my heart may become a tabernacle for Your presence, and a carrier of Your glory-fire.

END NOTES

[1] Brother Lawrence: *The Practice of the Presence of God*

[2] Jill Austin; *Visitations 1: The Epic of God's Heart*; Heidi Baker - Chariots of Fire *(Audio-CD: www.masterpotter.com 2004)*

Conclusion

Fire in the Desert is about our personal journey with God through the wilderness seasons in life, where our hearts can encounter Him and become a habitation for His presence. He is longing to revive our hearts, so our hearts can beat in rhythm with His heartbeat. He is calling His bride to come deeper with Him, to abide in the ocean of His presence, so she may ride with Him on the waves of His Spirit.

God has invited each one of us into a covenantal relationship with Him, but like all friendships, it comes with a price. Just as Jesus demonstrated His sacrificial love for us on the cross, so He is inviting you and me to lay down our lives for Him.

Sacrificial love involves yielding our hearts and lives to Him, as we daily offer ourselves as a love offering for Him. As we do this, we will discover He is more than enough to meet our needs, as we keep the eyes of our hearts on Him.

I pray God's fiery, passionate love will burn deep in your hearts and transform your inner beings. May you never give up, even in the turbulent seasons, but continue to pursue His face, as He draws you deeper into the chambers of His heart.

May you become one of His most beautiful vessels, full of His passionate love, radiating His fire and glory, as you heart becomes a tabernacle for His presence.

Fire in the Desert

Appendix A

BY THE AUTHOR

Kingdom Medicine Volume One begins a series of healing in the Kingdom by laying a foundation for the healing ministry. The *Foundation For Healing* is based on our intimacy with God and our ability to hear Him. It provides insights into some of the spiritual and emotional roots to sickness and disease. This book aims to encourage and empower the body of Christ to minister to one another in the area of healing, so healing becomes the norm in everyone's life. (2020)

Kingdom Medicine Volume Two provides a range of *Kingdom Tools* to assist in the healing and freedom ministry. The purpose of *Kingdom Tools* is to empower and equip the body of Christ with tools that can help identify the underlying issues, as well as provide ways to release healing and freedom. Different tools are used to provide freedom and healing, and the book describes in more depth the various tools that are available to treat the spiritual and emotional roots to sickness and disease (2020).

Kingdom Medicine Volume Three is *Divine Heart Surgery* and this is built upon already having a foundation for healing and the kingdom tools. *Divine Heart Surgery* requires coming into God's presence to assist the Great Surgeon as He operates on people's hearts. As we minister in His presence, we have the privilege of seeing what He does, as He delicately heals the wounded emotions and restores the traumatized areas of the heart. It involves additional tools including *Accessing the Courts of Heaven* and *Synchronising Areas of the Heart with Jesus*.

Into His Chambers is based on a vision that invites you to come deeper into the heart of God, by encountering the chambers of *Belonging, Identity, Suffering Heart of Christ* and *Anointing*. It is full of revelatory insight to help you go deeper in your relationship with God, including the power of His grace and the cross. It invites you to encounter His glory-presence in the Holy of Holies, and to become one who carries the heart of a prophet, priest, servant and king (2018).

At the peak of her medical career, Angela had a call on her life to work amongst the poor in Africa. What she didn't know was that God was going to derail her and take her down an unfamiliar path. As she obeyed God's call, she discovered another realm to sickness and disease; a realm that wasn't found in medical textbooks. Instead she received "on the job training" from the Great Physician Himself. This book combines faith with medicine, the supernatural with the natural and the physical with the emotional and spiritual, as you read the powerful testimonies and teachings on how to heal the sick, God's way! (2014).

Fire in the Desert

Appendix B

ABOUT THE AUTHOR

Angela Walker qualified as a doctor at Liverpool Medical School in 1991 and went on to pursue a career in Paediatrics and Child Health at the London teaching hospitals. She furthered her studies by taking a Master's degree in Clinical Paediatrics, followed by a Diploma in Tropical Medicine and Hygiene, before she went and served with Voluntary Services Oversees as a Paediatric lecturer in Uganda.

After becoming a Consultant in 2004, she studied at All Nations Bible College in Hertfordshire. Following this, she served with Iris Global for seven years on the mission field in Africa, where she practiced Kingdom Medicine. During this time, she discovered the possibility of there being spiritual and emotional roots to sickness and disease, and this prompted her to write her first book, 'Healing God's Way'.

She is an inspirational speaker, trainer, and pioneer with a passion to see hearts healed, people set free, lives transformed, and God's Kingdom advance in the nations. She is the founder and director of THEO Ministries.

For copies of her books or any enquiries, please visit the web or email:

www.theoministries.com
info@theoministries.com
www.amazon.com/author/drangelawalker

Fire in the Desert

Printed in Great Britain
by Amazon